SHALOM, SALAAM, PEACE

Allison Stokes
Study Guide by Pat Patterson

Quotations noted JPS are from *The TANAKH: The New JPS Translation According to the Traditional Hebrew Text.* Copyright 1985 by the Jewish Publication Society. Used by permission.

Quotations noted Qur'an are from *The Holy Qur'an: Arabic Text with English Translation and Commentary,* by Maulana Muhammad Ali. Dublin, Ohio: Ahmadiyya Anjuman Isha'at Islam Lahore Inc., 2002. (This English translation is a renowned classic of religious literature. It first appeared in 1917 and was the first English translation by a Muslim to be generally available and accessible in the West.)

Quotations noted NRSV are from the *New Revised Standard Version of the Bible,* copyright 1989 by the Division of Christian Education of the National Council of the Churches of Christ in the USA. Used by permission. All rights reserved.

Quotations noted RSV are from the *Revised Standard Version of the Bible,* copyright 1946, 1952, 1971 by the Division of Christian Education of the National Council of the Churches of Christ in the USA. Used by permission. All rights reserved.

Quotations noted KJV are from the King James or Authorized Version of the Bible.

ISBN 1-890569-98-4

LCCN: 2005936242

Printed in the United States of America

CONTENTS

PREFACE

Anew day is gently dawning, birds are singing exuberant praises, and with anticipation I reach for my laptop to begin the task before me. My assignment is to write a book about understandings of peace in Jewish, Muslim, and Christian traditions and about interreligious peacemaking. This challenge and my responsibility to my readers are awesome, yet I feel prepared.

At the time of this writing, I am an Ithaca College chaplain, ministering to the Protestant community. I have the privilege of working with chaplains from other faith traditions in a magnificent chapel designed for interreligious use. Our modern sanctuary, made of natural wood, stone, and glass, overlooks a beautiful pond. Although there are some six thousand people on campus, from this perspective who would know it? Observing the comings and goings of mallards, Canada geese, a blue heron, bunnies, a groundhog, and even deer provides regular distraction and occasional drama.

Across the chapel pond, on an island with a footbridge leading to it, is the peace pole the college community planted on September 11, 2002, and dedicated in an evening ceremony with candlelight encircling the pond. The setting is one of beauty and peace. It stands in contrast to all those places in our world that are devastated by war, barren, and unsafe. It is so exquisite that I do not forget to give thanks each day.

Because we chaplains share the sanctuary space, we must check in with one another regularly about our liturgical seasons and needs. Confronted with difference and the challenge of creating interfaith services and programming, we are constantly learning from one another. Not only do we work together as a chaplaincy team, we also serve together, along with faculty, staff, and students, on the college's Interfaith Council.

Interreligious dialogue is not new to me. From the time I began my ordained ministry in 1981, I have worked in multifaith, academic settings. Bringing people of different spiritual traditions together for mutual understanding and enlightenment is a lifetime commitment and passion.

When I am not on the job at the college, during my days off, and in the summers, I devote my energies to the Women's Interfaith Institute. By the time you read this book, however, I will have retired from college chaplaincy and my work will be exclusively with the Institute. I am the founding director of this nonprofit organization, which began in the Berkshire Hills of western Massachusetts in 1992 and branched out into the Finger Lakes of central New York in 2003. We are "women supporting women of diverse faiths in generating spiritual leadership, scholarship, and service."

In the summer of 2004, we opened the doors and dedicated our building in Seneca Falls, a historic church located in the same block as the Wesleyan Chapel. In 1848, the Wesleyan Chapel was the site of the first Women's Rights Convention under the leadership of Elizabeth Cady Stanton and a committee of like-minded women. The Women's Rights National Historical Park welcomes tourists from all over the world to Seneca Falls, "birthplace of women's rights."

The June weekend that we dedicated our Institute building, our theme was "Bringing Peace to Life." Festivities included planting a peace pole on our lawn like the one at Ithaca College. It is a conversation piece for passersby and a symbol of our commitment to bring peace to life. The words "May Peace Prevail on Earth" are inscribed on the pole in eight different languages—English, Arabic, Hebrew, Swahili, Chinese, Hindi, Spanish, and Seneca.[1]

The wisdom of Native Americans in keeping in mind the "seventh generation" (beyond their own) in their decision making and actions is an inspiration. For the sake of my grandchildren—Everleigh, Chase, Madison, Ruth, Jamie, and Baden—I labor for peace. Plato's observation that "Only the dead have seen the end of war" stands unrefuted by history. Will the living *never* see an end of war? From my perspective as an elder, no endeavor seems more imperative than better preparing the way for the peacemakers of the next generation.

Today faithful women and men everywhere are dedicated to being change agents. You will soon discover that I quote many of them in this book. I hope you will not find frequent quotations a distraction, but will read them carefully. Drawing on many sources or, to put it differently, inviting many voices to the discussion table, makes for rich conversation and understanding.

Although I intend for this study to be academically solid and intellectually challenging, I also want it to be accessible and appealing. And, although I strive to present material in a fair and balanced way, my perspective is necessarily limited and subjective. For these reasons, I do not hesitate to relate my own personal experiences when doing so seems appropriate and helps to make the point.

The mixing of scholarly material with personal narrative is an intentional approach to the subject that I would call feminist. Feminists are critical of writers who claim to be "objective," and/or to be normative for all; instead, they recognize that each person's perspective is necessarily limited by her or his context and experience. For this reason, feminists insist that those who would influence public opinion need to be clear about where they are coming from. You as a reader are sure to interact with this work in a personal way, because to the profound topic of "Shalom, Salaam, Peace" you will bring your own experiences, ideas, faith, and hopes.

I vividly remember being in college when in 1961 President John F. Kennedy launched the Peace Corps, declaring that *peace is the responsibility of our entire society.* He made his argument for peace not in geopolitical terms, but in human ones and so had a "hold on the imagination of a global generation."[2] Just months before a bullet took his life, JFK addressed human beings the world over:

> And if we cannot end now our differences, at least we can help make the world safe for diversity. For, in the final analysis, our most basic common link is that we all inhabit this small planet. We all breathe the same air. We all cherish our children's future. And we all are mortal.[3]

He reminded us that "our problems are man-made—therefore, they can be solved by man,"[4] and he moved us with his plea: "So let us persevere. Peace need not be impracticable, and war need not be inevitable."[5]

My hope, dear reader, is that the words I put to paper will be of benefit to you in your own peacemaking.

Shalom. Salaam. Peace.

> The Reverend Allison Stokes, Ph.D.
> Seneca Falls, New York
> Women's Equality Day—August 26, 2005

---

[1] Peace poles are made in Maple City, Michigan, by Peace Pole Makers USA. Planted by friends and organizations in front of schools, parks, churches, gardens, private homes, and city halls, they carry the message in over three hundred languages. Their Web site is *www.peacepoles.com.*

[2] These are the words of James Carroll in a remarkable piece, "JFK's November." This first appeared in the *Boston Globe* in November, 2003, forty years after Kennedy's death, and is reprinted in James Carroll, *Crusade: Chronicles of an Unjust War.* New York: Metropolitan Books, 2004, pp. 224-246.

[3] From "The Strategy of Peace," a major talk President Kennedy gave in June 1963 at American University, in Theodore C. Sorensen, ed. *"Let the Word Go Forth": The Speeches, Statements, and Writings of John F. Kennedy, 1947-1963.* New York: Delacorte Press, 1988, p. 286.

[4] Ibid., p. 283.

[5] Ibid., p. 284.

A NEW MILLENNIUM AND THE WORLDWIDE LONGING FOR PEACE

We need to find within ourselves the will to live by the values we proclaim—in our private lives, in our local and national societies, and in the world.

Kofi Annan¹

T he eve of a new millennium was near and the world, it seemed, was holding its breath. As 1999 drew to a close and 2000 approached, people marveled that we would be marking the passing of not just one year, ten years, or even one hundred years, but one *thousand* years. People were apprehensive. Could this happen peacefully? The time was right for terrorists to make a statement of raw power, to violently disrupt New Year celebrations with the attention of the world's population guaranteed. Police departments were on high alert in cities around the globe. In Times Square, security had never been tighter. Garbage cans were removed, manhole covers sealed.

For my extended family it was a time of particularly high anxiety. My brother, Harold, was the person with behind-the-scenes responsibility for the descent at midnight of the ball at One Times Square. Because of Harold's indispensable, if invisible, role, he was given a few passes for family members to attend a preview on December 30 of the Waterford crystal ball specially crafted for the occasion. What a thrill it was for me, with son, daughter-in-law, and two grandchildren, to pass through the Warner Brothers Studio Store and multilevels of security, take an elevator to the rooftop, and see the magnificent ball, six feet in diameter, with 504 crystal triangles and multicolored bulbs. Harold showed us the controller that he would use to begin the ball's sixty-second, seventy-seven-foot descent. He described the several practice runs and the mechanical backup system in case of electrical failure.

Harold was nervous, naturally—any mishap would be viewed worldwide. Although he would have preferred anonymity, his hometown paper learned of his role and ran a feature story. The reporter noted that as January 1 dawned, Harold would celebrate his forty-fifth birthday. (I remember well the happy night/morning of his birth: Dorothy, Christine, Vivian, and I had a *brother*.)

And then the day dawned. Hour after hour, as clocks struck midnight in the world's twenty-four time zones, television cameras captured joyous, tumultuous celebrations—a "rolling millennium" of magnificent fireworks displays and cultural events. There were no disruptions, no violence. With the anxious countdown over, the world's collective relief was palpable. Spirits soared. Television viewers the earth over marveled at the cultural and ethnic richness of festivities. At last it was Time Square's turn. At home in my living room I watched the giant crystal ball descend without incident, and I felt gratitude that with Harold's job successfully accomplished, I could let go and celebrate, too. Praise be!

The dawning of a third millennium created a focus, the achievements of communications technology brought us together, and for one short, twenty-four-hour period, we exuberantly experienced global human unity across difference. Anyone with access to a television set knew the earth truly as one "global village." Perhaps we could put behind us the bloody twentieth century during which forty-three million military personnel and sixty-two million civilians had perished.[2] Hopes were high that humanity was now ushering in a new time in the world's history.

I could not help but think of "On the Pulse of Morning," the poem that Maya Angelou wrote for President William Jefferson Clinton's inauguration in January 1993. Although the occasion was a new day in our country, its bright hopefulness felt just right for the world at the millennium. "Yet today I will call you to my riverside, / If you will study war no more," the poet wrote. One stanza in particular strikes me:

There is a true yearning to respond to
The singing River and the wise Rock.
So say the Asian, the Hispanic, the Jew
The African, the Native American, the Sioux,
The Catholic, the Muslim, the French, the Greek,
The Irish, the Rabbi, the Priest, the Sheik,
The Gay, the Straight, the Preacher,
The privileged, the homeless, the Teacher.
They hear. They all hear
The speaking of the Tree.[3]

The new millennium needed a global vision of the tree of life. Just weeks before New Year's Day, in December 1999, the Parliament of the World's Religions met in Cape Town, South Africa. A friend from the Women's Interfaith Institute and I were privileged to be among the some seven thousand people who gathered for ten days to hear lectures, attend seminars, enjoy music and dance concerts, view the AIDS quilt and other amazing exhibits, meet for interfaith dialogue, pray with religious traditions other than our own, and marvel at the glorious variety of dress, languages, foods, and faith represented. The peace flags that flew everywhere, made by children in South Africa's elementary schools, enhanced the celebratory mood. Our experience of human unity across difference was exhilarating.

Eight months later, in August 2000, a Millennium World Peace Summit of Religious and Spiritual Leaders was convened at the United Nations. About eight hundred leaders from around the globe as well as one thousand others attended this four-day meeting that had discussion of peace as its objective. While many wondered what lasting result might come of it, others observed that its primary value was simply allowing people of diverse religious backgrounds to meet and talk with one another. One participant, Rabbi Jonathan Sacks, Chief Rabbi of England, exclaimed:

God has brought us eyeball to eyeball with the diversity of His world....And right now he is asking us: Can we recognize God's image in someone who is not in my image? Can strangers, even enemies, become friends?[4]

Rabbi Sacks voiced what many were thinking—that religious leaders around the world often have real influence, even more than politicians. It was heartening then when they concluded the conference by signing a statement titled, "Commitment to Global Peace," and pledged to work with the United Nations and all men and women of goodwill toward peace.

Commenting on the unusual gathering of religious leaders, Lawrence E. Sullivan, the director of the Center for the Study of World Religions at Harvard, said, "I think the evidence is, they voted with their hearts in coming here." In an interview with Gustav Niebuhr, writer of *The New York Times'* Religion Journal, the educator noted: "If the religious people want to bring a new voice, they really have to go to school on the issues....Some of them have, most have not."[5]

The fervent hope for peace in the new millennium, which brought thousands of people to the World Parliament gathering in Cape Town and to the World Peace Summit of Religious and Spiritual Leaders in New York, was shattered by the horrific events of September 11, 2001. The destruction of the World Trade Center's twin towers and the attack on the Pentagon struck at the symbols of the United States' economic and military might. The deaths of thousands of innocent people brought an outpouring of world sympathy and support.

This support was short-lived, however. In early 2003, as it became apparent that the United States president was about to lead the country into a preemptive war on Iraq, citizens the world over felt outrage. Peace actions were planned. Organizers used the Internet, with the Web address *www.unitedforpeace.org*, as an efficient and powerful communications tool.

On February 15, 2003, coordinated antiwar demonstrations

took place in cities around the world—in Amsterdam, Barcelona, Cape Town, São Paulo, Ramallah, Bangkok, San Juan, Toronto, Istanbul, London, Manila, Jakarta, Warsaw, Athens, Berlin, Paris, Cairo, Tokyo, Rome, New York, and more. Individuals who had never before been activists, who had never before demonstrated, took to the streets to protest. Estimates were that as many as fifteen million people participated in the unprecedented "The World Says No to War" day. Any U.S. action, they said, would be unilateral. It would lack the support of the United Nations. Nonviolent means of settling the conflict had not been fully explored. War against Iraq would be an offensive, not a defensive, action. It could not be justified.

As massive as these demonstrations were, the will of the people went unacknowledged and unheeded. The president's mind had long been set. Dramatic "Shock and Awe" attacks began in March 2003.

A year later, on March 11, 2004, terrorists set off bombs in Barcelona, Spain, to protest the presence of Spanish troops serving in Iraq in support of the United States. This horror, destruction, and mayhem—the death of more innocents—made it clear that vulnerability to terrorism is a problem the entire world shares.

The response in Spain was phenomenal. An estimated eleven million citizens, or one-fourth of Spain's population, took to the streets. In shocked and angry protest, they demonstrated their overwhelming abhorrence of the attacks and their rejection of violence. They held up their palms, painted white, signifying innocent hands and insistence upon an alternative way to resolve conflict.

A student from Ithaca College, Jessica ("Jet") Murray, was there to witness the demonstrations. She sent a lengthy e-mail message to members of Students for a Just Peace, a campus organization, on March 23, 2004, telling about her experience. I quote in part:

> The people of Spain portrayed the most beautiful display of solidarity, hope and desire for peace I have ever seen. From my hostel above the Plaza [in Salamanca], I witnessed vigils

several times daily, public collective works of art, paper cranes, candles arranged in peace signs, banners, paintings. . .

The entire town gathered at night to hold silence...then march together around their city. This happened all over Spain, as I am sure you are aware. I am emailing to share with you the unified desire for peace I was lucky enough to witness....

Please use the tragic event as a pivotal one, to move from and point out to the world why peace is so necessary!

Keep me updated with your events!

Thinking of you all, Paz,

In the national election held in Spain one week after the Madrid attack, Prime Minister José María Aznar, a pro-Bush, Iraq war supporter, lost to Socialist Party challenger José Luis Rodríguez Zapatero. During the election campaign Zapatero had pledged to withdraw Spanish troops from Iraq, and on the day that he was sworn in as president, he did.

After 9/11, President Bush went out of his way, numerous times, to declare that the country is at war with terrorism—not with Islam. Terrorists who are ready and willing to take the lives of others and themselves in suicidal attacks are religious extremists. They are fanatics. Most Christians in the U.S. acknowledged that Muslims who murder innocents are not true representatives of Islam. But after 9/11, Christians also acknowledged their ignorance of Islam. So began a new effort—in churches, schools, government offices, the media, and peace organizations—to learn more about Islam. People are coming to believe that, in order for there to be world peace, intercultural and interreligious exchange and understanding are crucial.

This book is divided into three major sections. Section I examines the concept of peace in the three Abrahamic religions. Section II considers obstacles to breaking cycles of violence. Section III looks at keys to creating a world culture of peace. Section IV tells about women who are engaged in peacemaking, and a concluding chapter focuses on peacemakers' own inner peace through contemplative prayer.

One caveat. If this work appears Christocentric, readers should keep in mind the intention of *Shalom, Salaam, Peace*. It has been written by a Christian clergywoman primarily for Christian study and discussion. My efforts are in devotion to the Christ, who prayed "that they may all be one" (John 17:21). Jesus revealed God's extravagant, inclusive love. Facing death he prayed:

> Righteous Father, the world does not know you, but I know you; and these know that you have sent me. I made your name known to them, and I will make it known, so that the love with which you have loved me may be in them, and I in them." (John 17:25-26, NRSV)

Two millennia ago, Jesus himself longed for humanity's unity, for the oneness of all God's people. Through his teaching and example, he revealed that God's love, dwelling within us, is the way.

---

[1] Kofi Annan, "Do We Still Have Universal Values," in *Interreligious Insight: A journal of dialogue and engagement*, vol. 2, no. 3, July 2004, p. 15.

[2] Chris Hedges, *War Is a Force That Gives Us Meaning*. New York: Anchor Books, 2003, p. 13.

[3] Maya Angelou, *On the Pulse of Morning*. New York: Random House, 1993, n.p.

[4] Gustav Niebuhr, "Interfaith Meeting Tries to Build on Shared Goals," *The New York Times*, New York, Saturday, September 2, 2000, p. A15.

[5] Gustav Niebuhr, "World's Religious Figures Sign a Pledge for Peace," *The New York Times International*, September 1, 2000, p. A12.

PEACE AND THE ABRAHAMIC RELIGIONS

"We live now in days when Muslims, Jews, and Christians must return to their Scriptures with finer tools and a larger purpose, to lay a foundation for peace firmly grounded in each distinct tradition, but which also speaks to the heart's longing of their Abrahamic cousins, thereby appealing to our shared devotion to the one God."[1]

"Shalom." "Salaam." "Peace." The words for *peace* in Hebrew, Arabic, and English evoke the three, great world religions that are historically and spiritually linked. The number of people in the world who belong to each of these religions can only be estimated, but it is generally agreed that Christianity is the world's largest religion. There are about 2.1 billion Christians, 1.3 billion Muslims, and 14 million Jews. Together Christians (33 percent) and Muslims (21 percent) comprise more than half of the world's population.[2]

In the United States, Islam now shares with Judaism the status of the nation's second faith. While a statement of the family relationship among Judaism, Christianity, and Islam may seem elementary to some readers, it is important that we be on the same page before moving on to a discussion and analysis of the topic before us.

Jews, Christians, and Muslims believe in *one God*: all are "monotheistic" religions. There are not many gods, as in some faith traditions, but one creator, one supreme being who acts in human history.

Jews, Christians, and Muslims all honor Abraham as spiritual ancestor, as the founding father of their faith. For this reason, the three religions are increasingly being known as the "Abrahamic" religions. The story of Abraham and Sarah, who heard the call of the Lord and set out in faith for a new land, is a shared story:

> The LORD to Abram, "Go forth from your native land and from your father's house to the land that I will show you.
> I will make of you a great nation,
> And I will bless you;
> I will make your name great,
> And you shall be a blessing.
> I will bless those who bless you
> And curse him that curses you;
> And all the families of the earth
> Shall bless themselves by you." (Genesis 12:1-3, JPS)

The Genesis story is found in the Hebrew Scriptures, which are sacred to Jews, Christians, and Muslims. Jews call the ancient Bible, the Hebrew Scriptures, the "Tanakh" (tah-NAKH). As my father taught me when he was my fifth-grade Sunday school teacher, the Tanakh is comprised of three parts: the *Torah* (the five books of Moses), the *Nevi'im* (the prophets) and the *Kethuvim* (the writings).

Christians embrace the Hebrew Scriptures as their own, referring to them as the "Old Testament." In a day of increased religious sensitivity, however, some Christians intentionally avoid speaking of the "Old Testament," because this implies the Hebrew Scriptures are obsolete. For Jews, they are the only Holy Scriptures. For Muslims, the Hebrew Scriptures and the New Testament are revealed by God and holy, but they are superseded by the Holy Qur'an—God's revelation to Muhammad.

It is important to know that the Bible and the Qur'an differ in how they tell the common stories and in the interpretations they draw. Readers of the Jewish and Christian Scriptures will find familiar figures in the Qur'an—Abraham, Moses, David, John the Baptist, Jesus, and Mary—but the stories differ, sometimes radically. For example, in the Qur'an Ibrahim is prepared to sacrifice not Isaac, his son by Sarah, but Ishmael, his son by Hagar. (Islamic tradition traces Arab genealogy, and Muhammad's prophethood, through Ishmael.) Jon D. Levenson, professor of Jewish Studies at Harvard University, observes that the Muslim attitude toward both testaments of the Christian Bible traditionally runs a spectrum that ranges from respect to a charge that large parts of them are forgeries. The Qur'an, he writes, goes out of its way to deny that Jesus died on the cross.

Like the Bible, the Qur'an is divided into chapters and verses. The 114 chapters are known as *suras.* An early *sura* of the Qur'an makes explicit the place of earlier Jewish and Christian Scripture in Islam:

> I, Allāh, am the best Knower, Allāh, (there is) no god but He, the Ever-living, the Self-subsisting, by Whom all subsist. He has revealed to thee the Book with truth, verifying that which is before it, and He revealed the Torah and the Gospel. (3:1-3, Qur'an)

The "thee" in this passage is Muhammad, Messenger of Allah, who lived some six hundred years after Jesus. Muslims refer to their fellow Jewish and Christian monotheists as "People of the Book," and for Muslims the Book is the word of Allah himself. With the exception of Christian fundamentalists, Jews and Christians regard biblical text as written by divinely inspired human authors, rather than humans who took dictation from God. Muslims, however, regard the Qur'an, which means "The Recitation," as the eternal word of Allah. Muhammad, God's Messenger, served as conduit. Because the language of God's original revelation is Arabic, translations of the Qur'an are considered mere interpretations.

To help Christians understand just how differently Muslims view their sacred scripture, one scholar has explained that the Qur'an does not correspond to the Bible, but to Christ himself, as the *logos,* or eternal word of the Father. "In short, if Christ is the word made flesh, the Qur'an is the word made book." Another scholar makes the point differently, saying that to hear the Qur'an recited and to take the words into oneself through prayer "is to experience the presence of God with the same kind of intimacy as Catholics feel when they receive Christ as consecrated bread and wine at mass."[3]

The five pillars of Islam are comprised of the practices of declaring faith, prayer, fasting, charity, and pilgrimage. The first of the five pillars of Islam is the Oneness of God. "Surely your God is One" (37:4, Qur'an) is a message proclaimed throughout the Holy Qur'an. Each of the 114 suras, with the exception of one, begins with the verse: "In the name of Allāh, the Beneficent, the Merciful." Sura 112 is considered by Muslims to be the essence of monotheism. This short, four-verse sura reads:

In the name of Allāh, the Beneficent, the Merciful.

Say: He, Allāh, is One. Allāh is He on Whom all depend. He begets not, nor is He begotten; And none is like Him.

The Shema is the passage from the Torah that makes the celebrated affirmation that God is One:

Hear, O Israel! The LORD is our God, the LORD alone. You shall love the LORD your God with all your heart and with all your soul and with all your might. Take to heart these instructions with which I charge you this day. Impress them upon your children. Recite them when you stay at home and when you are away, when you lie down and when you get up. Bind them as a sign on your hand and let them serve as a symbol on your forehead; inscribe them on the doorposts of your house and on your gates. (Deuteronomy 6:4-9, JPS)

In Jewish tradition these verses are known as the Shema because the first word, hear, is *shema* in Hebrew. Jews place the words of the Shema on the doorpost at the entrance to their homes, in a *mezuzah*, and also in the entrance to synagogues and temples, signifying that they are to constantly guide one's thought and action.

According to Mark's Gospel, when Jesus was asked, "Which commandment is the first of all?" he answered:

The first is, "Hear, O Israel: the Lord our God, the Lord is one; you shall love the Lord your God with all your heart, and with all your soul, and with all your mind, and with all your strength." (Mark 12:29-30, NRSV)

Christians affirm God's oneness, at the same time professing their belief that the one God is known (or experienced) in three persons, the persons of the Trinity: Father, Son, and Holy Spirit. Seeking to move beyond gender to Spirit, many Christians today prefer to speak of "Creator, Christ, and Comforter," or "Creator, Redeemer, and Sustainer." When Christians use the words of the Nicene Creed, they begin by saying, "We believe in one God. . . ." They then name belief in "God the Father"; "in one Lord, Jesus Christ, the only Son of God"; and "in the Holy Spirit, the Lord, the giver of life, who proceeds from the Father and the Son, who with the Father and the Son is worshiped and glorified."

Jews and Muslims cannot accept Trinitarian belief, which is contrary to their understanding of monotheism. Jews and Muslims view Jesus as a prophet of God, not the Christ, or Messiah, and certainly not "One with the Father," as in Christian conviction. For most Jews and Muslims such a claim is incomprehensible, even idolatrous. (More will be said about the Muslim critique in Chapter 4.)

No matter how they are described—as the monotheistic religions, as the Abrahamic religions, or as People of the Book—Judaism, Christianity, and Islam are inextricably linked as family. A key difference is that Judaism is not a proselytizing, or missionary, faith. In contrast, Christianity and Islam share a zeal to expand by conversion. Today, competition between Islam and Christianity is most dramatic in Africa as missionaries seek to win converts.

The three chapters that follow in this section will focus on the texts and concept of peace in the three religions: "shalom" in the Hebrew Scriptures, "salaam" in the Holy Qur'an and Islam, and the "peace of Jesus Christ" in the Christian Scriptures. In considering the distinctive concepts for peace, we will necessarily consider their distinctive understandings of the nature of God—the One

5

known to Jews as LORD (the conventional English rendering of the four-letter Hebrew name YHWH), to Muslims as Allah, and to Christians as triune God.

---

[1] *Waging Peace: A Two-part Discussion of Religion-based Peacemaking.* Sponsored by Washington National Cathedral and the United States Institute of Peace. Washington, D.C.: Washington National Cathedral, April, 2003, p. 58.

[2] *www.adherents.com/Religions_By_Adherents.html.*

[3] See "The Bible and the Qur'an: Searching the Holy Books for Roots of Conflict & Seeds of Reconciliation," by Kenneth L. Woodward, in *Newsweek,* February 11, 2002, p. 54.

1

SHALOM, THE LORD,
AND THE TANAKH

As I gather up my things and prepare to leave my office on Friday afternoons, I anticipate with pleasure what has become a kind of ritual between us. Michael is sitting on the couch in his office next door, reading and quietly readying himself for the service soon to come. His door is open and I look in. "*Shabbat shalom*," I say with a big smile. "*Shabbat shalom*," he warmly replies. "Have a good weekend." "You, too."

Why should this small, apparently insignificant exchange bring me such delight?

I think it is because, for a brief moment, I am entering Michael's world. "*Shabbat shalom*." I speak a greeting in a language I do not know. I acknowledge a sabbath that is not my own. Difference between Christian and Jew is bridged in a small way... and I experience Shalom.

In my younger years I was a great fan of the Broadway musical *Milk and Honey*. As I did housework I played the LP record over and over, listening especially for the upbeat song "Shalom." I loved to sing along. The lyrics, by Jerry Herman, describe in a light and engaging way the various uses and meanings of the Hebrew word for *peace*.

Shalom, Shalom,
You'll find Shalom,
The nicest greeting you know;
It means bonjour, salud,
And skoal and twice as much hello.
It means a million lovely things,
Like peace be yours, welcome home.
And even when you say goodbye,

You say goodbye with Shalom.
It's a very useful word,
It can hardly go wrong.
This is your home as long as you say:
Shalom, the nicest greeting I know;
Shalom, means twice as much as hello.
It means a million lovely things,
Like peace be yours, welcome home.
And even when you say goodbye,
If your voice has "I don't want to go" in it,
Say goodbye with a little "hello" in it
And say goodbye with Shalom.[1]

The word "*shalom*" appears in the Tanakh hundreds of times. Its meaning, as Herman's song makes clear, is broad. Implied in *shalom* is wholeness—a oneness, or right relation, between the Lord, creation, and humanity. The prophet Isaiah gives compelling images of peaceful coexistence. We read in an early chapter of Isaiah the vision of a coming day when "a shoot shall grow out of the stump of Jesse":

The wolf shall dwell with the lamb,
The leopard lie down with the kid;
The calf, the beast of prey, and the fatling together,
With a little boy to herd them.
The cow and the bear shall graze,
Their young shall lie down together;
And the lion, like the ox, shall eat straw.
A babe shall play
Over a viper's hole,
And an infant pass his hand
Over an adder's den.
In all of My sacred mount

Nothing evil or vile shall be done;
For the land shall be filled with devotion to the Lord
As water covers the sea.   (Isaiah 11:6-9, JPS)

A portion of this poem appears again in a closing chapter of Isaiah. The Lord is "creating a new heaven and a new earth; the former things shall not be remembered, they shall never come to mind" (65:17, JPS). The new Jerusalem will be a return to the first creation, a peaceful kingdom:

The wolf and the lamb shall graze together,
And the lion shall eat straw like the ox,
And the serpent's food shall be earth.
In all My sacred mount
Nothing evil or vile shall be done.   (65:25, JPS)

Here is a picture of serenity and safety. There are no predators, no prey. The weak are not threatened by the powerful. This future of harmony and well-being for all, a new heaven and a new earth, stirred the imagination of artist Edward Hicks. In the center of his famous painting of the Bible's "Peaceable Kingdom" (ca. 1830–1835), a large lion stands staring into the distance with wide and almost startled eyes. The beast is head to head with an ox, and at their feet a lamb is curled up.[2]

Another Edward Hicks rendering of the peaceable kingdom, "The Peaceable Kingdom of the Branch," depicts a young child, with an arm draped easily over the head of a lion, looking outward toward the viewer. The lion nestles close to the child's side, and at the child's feet a sheep rests its head on the head of a wolf. The image is one of safety and security for the weak. But that's not all. If the viewer looks carefully, she can see a lovely tableau in the distance. By a stream, under a huge natural bridge and a canopy of trees, four Native Americans are engaged in conversation with four Englishmen. The artist wants us to understand that the peaceable kingdom will bring a new day in human relations: enemies are reconciled, difference is bridged, harmony prevails.[3]

Such is the image or concept of shalom in the Hebrew Scriptures. Shalom is about right relations—with the Lord, with one's fellow human beings, with creation. As the Lord's chosen people, the Hebrews lived in covenant with the Lord. After Moses led the Hebrew people out of their captivity in Egypt, after receiving God's gift of the commandments and wandering with them in the wilderness for forty years, and when he knew he would not be crossing over with his people into the Promised Land, Moses spoke to them in a final address:

> I call heaven and earth to witness against you this day: I have put before you life and death, blessing and curse. Choose life—if you and your offspring would live—by loving the Lord your God, heeding His commands, and holding fast to Him. For thereby you shall have life and shall long endure upon the soil that the Lord your God swore to your ancestors, Abraham, Isaac, and Jacob, to give to them.   (Deuteronomy 30:19-20, JPS)

To be a seeker of peace is to make a choice for the good and for life. The Hebrew prophets who followed Moses made quite clear what the Lord required of the people. They were to live by the Torah. They were "to do justice and to love goodness, and to walk modestly with your God" (Micah 6:8, JPS).

In the Hebrew Scriptures, shalom is a gift from God, inclusive of all creation, grounded in salvation and covenantal fidelity, and inextricably bound up with justice.[4] Amos spoke for the Lord, warning the people:

> I loathe, I spurn your festivals,
> I am not appeased by your solemn assemblies,
> If you offer Me burnt offerings—or your meal offerings—
> I will not accept them:
> I will pay no heed.
> To your gifts of fatlings.
> Spare Me the sound of your hymns,
> And let Me not hear the music of your lutes.
> But let justice well up like water,
> Righteousness like an unfailing stream.   (Amos 5:21-24, JPS)

Psalm 34 instructs:
Come, O children, listen to me;
    I will teach you the fear of the Lord.
Which of you desires life,
    and covets many days to enjoy good?
Keep your tongue from evil,
    and your lips from speaking deceit.
Depart from evil, and do good;
        seek peace, and pursue it.
The eyes of the Lord are on the righteous,
    and his ears are open to their cry.   (Psalm 34:11-15, NRSV)

In our time the ancient dispute between Israelis and Palestinians over the Promised Land continues to resist the best efforts of peacemakers. One mother describes the peace that Israelis and Palestinians yearn for:

Peace is the feeling that you are not threatened, that your children are not threatened and that your grandchildren might live in a peaceful environment. When you don't have to worry about your children going out, whether they will come back safe. This is the peace we seek.[5]

But this peace is elusive. In recent years the use by the Israelis of their superior military power over the Palestinians has provoked much criticism of Israeli military actions. Swift and overwhelming Israeli retaliation against Palestinians for acts of violence, particularly suicide bombings, has led to condemnation of the Israeli's disproportionate use of force.

Many Christians are taught that the New Testament is superior to the Hebrew Bible, that many of the laws in the Hebrew Bible are outdated, and that Jesus taught another, better way. An example of Hebrew morality that is often criticized is the "eye for an eye" policy of retributive justice. Quoting Mohandas Gandhi, people will say, "An eye for an eye leaves the whole world blind."

The criticism of this biblical teaching, however, is taken out of historical context. The Christian interpretation of the commandment in Leviticus assumes that it encourages bloody, retributive justice. The fact is, in a time when societies were not bound by a rule of law, when the typical form of justice was clan vengeance, the "eye for an eye" law was actually an effort to limit excessive retaliation and revenge. It was a refinement of justice, meant to serve as a limitation on what kind of response an injured party could give. According to the Torah, the Lord spoke to Moses, who instructed the people, saying:

> If anyone kills any human being, he shall be put to death. One who kills a beast shall make restitution for it: life for life. If anyone maims his fellow, as he has done so shall it be done to him: fracture for fracture, eye for eye, tooth for tooth. The injury he inflicted on another shall be inflicted on him. . . . You shall have one standard for stranger and citizen alike: for I the Lord am your God." (Leviticus 24:17-22, JPS)

One standard for stranger and citizen alike represented a higher ethic, an advance.

In invoking images of peace and justice, the poetry of the Hebrew Scriptures is unsurpassed. I recall a Sunday service at the Vassar College Chapel in the mid-eighties when the threat of a nuclear nightmare loomed large in the public consciousness and the nuclear disarmament movement was at its peak. Our guest preacher focused his message on a peace theme. As the service ended and we began to process down the aisle together, I turned to him and asked if he would like to give the benediction. He opened the Bible in his hand, hurriedly leafed through its pages and found the precise passage he was looking for. When the hymn was over, he raised his hand in the familiar sign of blessing and read with gladness in his voice:

> For you shall go out in joy,
>   and be led back in peace;
> the mountains and the hills before you

shall burst into song,
and all the trees of the field shall clap their hands.

(Isaiah 55:12, NRSV)

Yes. YES! The words were perfect. In faith we could set aside fears and instead know our Creator's divine blessing. It was a moment of shalom I have not forgotten.

After 9/11, Rabbi Arthur Waskow, director of the Shalom Center in Philadelphia, wrote a remarkable article, "We All Live in a Sukkah." Here he explains the Jewish harvest festival of Sukkot, when families and organizations celebrate by building a sukkah. A sukkah is a fragile hut with a roof that is leafy and leaky. It is vulnerable, lasting only a week, letting in starlight, wind, and rain. In evening Sukkot prayers, Jews ask God—"*Ufros alenu sukkat shomekha*"—"Spread over all of us your sukkah of shalom."

Rabbi Waskow notes that the prayer is not for a tent, house, or palace of peace, but a sukkah of peace because a sukkah is vulnerable. We try to achieve peace and safety by building with steel and concrete and toughness, but the sukkah comes to remind us that we are vulnerable. On September 11, "the ancient truth came home: We all live in a sukkah."

There are only wispy walls and leaky roofs between us. The planet is in fact one interwoven web of life. The command to love my neighbor as I do myself is not an admonition to be nice: It is a statement of truth like the law of gravity. For my neighbor and myself are interwoven.[6]

Rabbi Waskow wonders—how can we make our vulnerable planet into a place of shalom, of peace and security, harmony and wholeness? He answers that it is only by recognizing that we all are vulnerable and by becoming a world where all communities feel responsible to all other communities.

"Spread over all of us your sukkah of shalom." *Ufros alenu sukkat shomekha.*

[1] "Shalom" music and lyrics by Jerry Herman. Copyright © 1961 by Jerry Herman. Sheet Music, Edwin H. Morris & Company, a Division of MPL Communications, Inc.

[2] This Hicks painting is in the Fenimore Art Museum in Cooperstown, New York.

[3] This Hicks oil on canvas (Bucks County, Pennsylvania, 1830–1840) can be viewed in Colonial Williamsburg's Abby Aldrich Rockefeller Folk Art Center in Williamsburg, Virginia.

[4] The National Conference of Catholic Bishops make this point in their pastoral letter on war and peace—"The Challenge of Peace: God's Promise and Our Response." For more about the pastoral letter, see my discussion in the next chapter.

[5] Shair Dajani quoted in Ann N. Madsen, *Making Their Own Peace: Twelve Women of Jerusalem*. New York: Lantern Books, 2003, p. 170.

[6] The article is found in *From the Ashes: A Spiritual Response to the Attack on America*. From the editors of Beliefnet. Rodale, 2001, p. 215.

2

SALAAM, ALLAH, AND THE HOLY QUR'AN

"Assalamu Alykum!"

My young Muslim friend's greeting is always the same. Whether in person or in an e-mail message, Himmatilla begins with the Arabic, *"Assalamu Alykum."* Peace be upon you.

During his time as a student at Ithaca College, this dear young man from Uzbekistan won my heart. We both looked forward to our time together when he would tell me about his faith. He was so earnest and eloquent, too, even though English was his second language—third, actually.

The word *Islam* means "peace," he explained, or is derived from the word for peace. Himmatilla was passionate in his desire for peace between people and nations; unfortunately he felt that many of his friends do not understand his ideas. Just as he was to leave New York to return to his country, in August 2003, he wrote to me:

I believe God will reward you for your beautiful intentions. That is how people differ from each other, according to their intentions and by their wishes and ambitions. You can ask someone what his/her ambition is and tell what kind of person he is. I know you wish peace and better life for everyone, and I wish you to achieve that....

We are all human beings and we all have the same problems: our next generations are going to face ecological, psychological and social problems, and most of them will arise from the mistakes done today by us, by today's people. So, we have

15

to come together and discuss things. We have to find common solutions. We have to put aside religious differences, race differences, class differences and any other differences which put us apart from each other. We shouldn't be ignorant about each other. This increases the gap between people and they start "guessing" about each other, which obviously leads to misguidance. We have so many Ones: One planet, One future, One nature, One origin, One heart. Why do we have to misunderstand each other and blame each other in our own mistakes? Why do we have to put mountains between us? I believe the future will be different and there will be people who will be strong in their faiths and they will be as a bridge between any other differences... for the sake of Allah and no other intentions.

I believe you will be one of them because you intend to put a bridge between people of different faiths. May Allah bless you for your intention.

This e-mail message touched me deeply, for despite our differences in age, gender, religion, and national origin, I understood Himmatilla, and I felt understood by him. In our mutual respect and care for each other, I felt Allah's peace upon us. I felt the peace that passes all understanding. And I hope one day to see my friend again, *Insha'Allah* (God willing).

As Himmatilla was eager for me to understand, salaam is central to the faith. In the words of a Muslim scholar:

Peace and Islam are derived from the same root and may be considered synonymous. One of God's names is Peace. The concluding words of the daily prayers of every Muslim are words of peace. The greeting of the Muslims when they return to God is peace. The daily salutations among the Muslims are expressions of peace. The adjective "Muslim" means, in a sense, peaceful. Heaven in Islam is the abode of peace.

This is how fundamental and dominant the theme of peace is in Islam.[1]

Like his passion for peace, Himmatilla's emphasis on good intention, on righteousness, is also integral to the faith, not something idiosyncratic to him. A Muslim is "one who submits." In Islam, the straight path, submission to the will of Allah is the most important virtue; and the Qur'an is a comprehensive guide for those who seek to know and do the will of Allah.

Allah is the Arabic name for God that all Arabic speakers use—whether Jew, Christian, or Muslim. How much misunderstanding could be avoided if more Christians knew that all Arabic-speaking people know God as Allah? In order to help bridge our differences, today more Muslims are substituting the word *God* for Allah in conversing with Christians. (For more about Allah and God, see my discussion in the next chapter of the question "Do Christians and Muslims worship the same God?")

The events of September 11 and the U.S. invasions of Afghanistan and Iraq caused Christians in America who knew little about Islamic religion and history to learn more. As a result, many of us are now more informed than we once were; and we understand that just as in Christianity, there is a wide diversity in Islamic faith and culture.

Particular attention has been focused on the meaning of the word *jihad*. Was the attack on the United States a jihad, a holy war? While Muslim terrorists view their suicidal attacks as jihad, most Muslims believe terrorism is an unacceptable strategy used by radical Islamists. They explain that *jihad* in Arabic means "striving" or "effort" and that true jihad is the personal effort or striving to live more faithfully. The twisted mission of terrorists is a misinterpretation of the Qur'an's meaning.

Fighting in defense is allowed in Islam. The Qur'an states: "And fight in the way of Allāh against those who fight against you but be not aggressive. Surely Allāh loves not the aggressors" (2:190, Qur'an). In his commentary on this text, Maulana Muhammad Ali explains that "fighting in the way of Allāh" means fighting defensively. Muslims are allowed to take up the sword only as a measure of self-defense. A related text he cites in his commentary is, "Permission (to fight) is given to those on whom war is made, because they are oppressed..." (22:39, Qur'an). According to this learned scholar, "Fighting for the propagation of the faith is not once mentioned in the whole of the Qur'an."[2] In fact, the Qur'an asserts "there is no compulsion in religion..." (2:256, Qur'an). This verse is viewed as sufficient answer to those who claim that the Prophet offered Islam or the sword as alternatives.

Even though the Qur'an places far more emphasis on acts of justice, mercy, and compassion than upon verses that call for jihad against the infidels, and even though these are few in number, they are much quoted and have "fired Muslim zealots in every age," according to journalist Kenneth Woodward.[3] And Harvard's Jon Levenson observes:

> Although a cottage industry has sprung up to define jihad exclusively as an internal struggle to gain self-mastery in order to act morally, the classic Muslim tradition also uses the term to denote war against unbelievers to extend the territory governed by Islam (an idea not without its historical analogues in Christianity and Judaism).[4]

Unlike Jesus, Muhammad became the military and political leader of an emerging community of believers. During his lifetime, he led a great religious movement. For Christians to understand Muslim perspectives, a key is understanding the difference between the lives of Jesus and Muhammad.

In the 600s C.E., before Muhammad began to preach, the tribes of the Arabian Desert were continually engaged in fierce and bloody war. Arabia was a lawless land where the people worshiped many gods and prayed to idols. Muhammad's achievement in founding Islam was in bringing the message of one God and replacing the old loyalty to tribes with a new community, or *umma*, of equality and brotherhood. As a statesman, Muhammad was able to unite his people, make his religious message into law, and establish *pax Islamica*—Islamic peace.

For Muslims, Muhammad is not divine, but he is the perfect person. He is to be emulated because he was able to balance living in the real world with the principles of religion. Although Muslims undoubtedly honor Jesus as a prophet, they do not view him as a model for living.

For me, insight into the Muslim perspective on Jesus came from an unexpected source. I found in the library of my late grandfather, the Reverend Dr. Oscar E. Allison, a United Methodist clergyman, an interesting volume entitled, *The Young Moslem Looks at Life*. This book, published in 1937, was written by Murray T. Titus, who began serving as a Christian missionary to Muslims in North India in 1910, after earning degrees from Ohio Wesleyan University and the Hartford Seminary Foundation. Although his Christian bias is quite apparent and the work is dated, Dr. Titus was well acquainted with Muslim ideas of Christianity; and his book is useful, even today. He presents a sensitive and sympathetic view of Islam and the faith of young Muslims.

From his own experience, the missionary explains how Muslims (or "Moslems") regard Jesus:

[Jesus] did not live a practical, well rounded life full of activity. He was not a man of affairs, nor the founder of a great nation, nor a lawgiver, nor a king, nor the leader of great armies. On the contrary, he was a meek and humble ascetic who renounced the world and its lusts, never married, and knew nothing of the problems of business or family life and the rearing of children. With such a limited range of human experience, how can Jesus be considered the ideal man?[5]

From the perspective of Muslims, the teaching of Jesus is highly impractical, says Dr. Titus:

How can one live up to his standards? Non-resistance to evil; turning the other cheek; going the second mile; praying for one's enemies; and maintaining purity not only in action but in the heart as well! How can such things be? After all, this is a life of flesh and blood we live, and man cannot be expected to accomplish the impossible. Christianity . . . makes no provision for the weakness of the flesh. Islam does. Christian ideals are unattainable and unworkable. Islam is easy and workable.[6]

Islam aims for a middle position, a "greater balance." A contemporary Muslim scholar, Akbar S. Ahmed, explains:

The ideal Muslim is the Prophet himself, leading the prayer in the mosque, the army in the battlefield, the council of elders as they discussed matters of state. His successors, the caliphs— and indeed all Muslim rulers—have tried to follow this model.[7]

Muslims believe that the Prophet Muhammad is the last prophet, and the Book revealed to him is to be a source of guidance for all time. All that needs to be revealed is revealed. Muslims believe that theirs is the last and final path to God, although there are other paths, which may also be valid. Indeed, the Qur'an goes out of its way to emphasize that Christians and Jews—the people of the Book—are to be treated with special respect.

A contemporary writer and scholar who is doing heroic service in helping Jews and Christians to understand Islam and Muhammad's accomplishment is Karen Armstrong. She is dedicated to building bridges between Islam and the West, to shining light on the long history of the West's "entrenched cultural prejudice toward the Muslim faith." This has not been easy. As she was working on a biography of the Prophet, at about the time of Ayatollah Khomeini's infamous *fatwa* against Salman Rushdie for *The Satanic Verses*, finding a publisher was not easy. Many editors thought that Muslims would find it intolerable that a Western woman would dare to write about their revered Prophet. But this was not the case. After the book was published, Armstrong was moved by the generous response of Muslims in Europe, the United States, and in the Islamic world:

Far from reacting in the knee-jerk way that many of my Western friends had darkly foretold, Muslims took both me and my book to their hearts, and I found that I had made a host of new friends. It is a tribute to Muslims and to the tolerance of their religion that they could respond so positively at such a frightening time.[8]

Karen Armstrong believes that any reader can benefit from learning about Muhammad, and I agree. I highly recommend *Muhammad: A Biography of the Prophet.* Here we learn that the Western image of Muhammad as cold, cruel, and vengeful is very different from the real story. The notion that Islam is a religion based upon the sword is a Western myth and the root of much prejudice. Armstrong's chapter, "Holy Peace," is a particularly compelling account of the Prophet's peaceful conquest of Mecca in 630, achieved without bloodshed two years before his death. Of the Prophet she writes:

> In our war-torn world, Muhammad reminds us that making peace is not simply a matter of signing on the dotted line or shaking hands on the White House lawn. Peacemaking is often dangerous and frightening; it requires all our resources of imagination and originality. It means that we must leave old certainties and securities behind and migrate to a risky, unknown future; that there might well be a moment, as there was in the Prophet's life, when the only possible solution is to lay aside the armed struggle, to desist from retaliation, and embrace a courageous policy of nonviolence; and that a lasting peace must be based on justice and a genuine respect for the sacred rights of others.[9]

Karen Armstrong is a person who is working for lasting peace based on justice and respect for the rights of others. She has a remarkable story of spiritual discovery. During the early sixties, at the age of seventeen, she entered a convent where she spent seven years as a Roman Catholic nun before leaving her order and becoming a writer, lecturer, and interpreter of religion.[10] Through her scholarship she seeks to promote interfaith understanding and to dispel prejudice.

Armstrong has sought to enter into the minds of the Crusaders "so that we can understand what they thought they were doing

21

when they slaughtered Muslims and Jews as an act of the love of God."[11] In her view, bad relations have existed between the Abrahamic religions ever since the Crusades; and the journey toward understanding and peace will take all of us a long time.

Yes, the legacy of the Crusades is still very much in our collective conscience. This was apparent in the public outcry against President Bush's use of the word *crusade* in an early reference to the United States's invasion of Iraq.[12] That he had to desist from such language and insist that the war is not against Islam marks a step forward.

---

[1] Hammudah Abdalati, *Islam in Focus.* Plainfield, Indiana: American Trust Publications, 1996, pp. 36-37.

[2] *The Holy Qur'an.* Ohio: Ahmadiyya Anjuman Isha'at Islam Lahore Inc. USA, 2002, p. 85, note 190a.

[3] "The Bible and the Qur'an: Searching the Holy Books for Roots of Conflict and Seeds of Reconciliation." *Newsweek.* February 11, 2003, p. 52.

[4] Jon D. Levenson, "Do Christians and Muslims worship the same God?" *The Christian Century,* April 20, 2004, p. 33.

[5] Murray T. Titus, *The Young Moslem Looks at Life.* New York: Friendship Press, 1937, p. 133.

[6] Ibid., pp. 133-134.

[7] Akbar S. Ahmed, *Islam Today.* New York: I. B. Tauris Publishers, 2002, p. 27.

[8] Karen Armstrong, *Muhammad: A Biography of the Prophet.* HarperSanFrancisco, 1993, p. 6.

[9] Ibid., p. 8.

[10] See Armstrong's book, *Through the Narrow Gate: A Memoir of Spiritual Discovery.* New York: St. Martin's Press, 1994, 2005.

[11] Karen Armstrong, *Holy War: The Crusades and Their Impact on Today's World.* New York: Anchor Books, 2001, p. xvi.

[12] On Sunday, September 16, 2001, the president remarked, "This crusade, this war on terrorism, is going to take a while." *www.csmonitor.com/2001/0919*

3

THE PEACE OF CHRIST,
THE TRIUNE GOD,
AND THE NEW TESTAMENT

"Peace be with you."

"And also with you."

During the time in the Christian service or mass known as the "Greeting of Peace," these are the words that are exchanged, along with handshakes or warm hugs. In this simple, ritual formula, worshipers share the peace bestowed by the risen Christ and also symbolically make peace— establish right relation—with their neighbors before approaching God. As a sign of reconciliation, the greeting of peace derives from Jesus' words recorded in the Gospel of Matthew:

So when you are offering your gift at the altar, if you remember that your brother or sister has something against you, leave your gift there before the altar and go; first be reconciled to your brother or sister, and then come and offer your gift.

(5:23-24, NRSV)

The exchange of the peace is a practice that dates back to the first Christians. One greeted another with a "holy kiss." References to it are made in Romans 16:16; 1 Corinthians 16:20; 2 Corinthians 13:12; 1 Thessalonians 5:26; and 1 Peter 5:14. In the early church, an unwillingness to exchange the peace with any of the assembled disqualified one from receiving communion.[1] In modern liturgical practice, the greeting is placed either before the morning offering or before the Eucharist (Holy Communion). Increasingly, however, it is becoming common practice for congregations to open worship with an exuberant greeting of peace—to the delight of many and the uneasiness of some.

Jesus' birth gave the Hebrew notion of shalom a changed meaning. Our discussion of the Christian understanding of peace begins with Isaiah's proclamation:

> For to us a child is born,
>> to us a son is given;
> and the government will be upon his shoulder,
>> and his name will be called
> "Wonderful Counselor, Mighty God,
>> Everlasting Father, Prince of Peace."   (Isaiah 9:6, RSV)

Christians embrace Jesus as the "Prince of Peace," the Christ. We speak of our faith in an incarnate God—God with us, "Emmanuel." Jesus Christ is the Word of God made flesh. At his birth "a multitude of the heavenly host" appeared to shepherds in the fields "praising God and saying, 'Glory to God in the highest heaven, and on earth peace among those whom he favors'" (Luke 2:13-14, NRSV).

The Prince of Peace taught the things that make for peace. He was a revolutionary, challenging the received moral and ethical wisdom of the past:

> You have heard that it was said, "An eye for an eye and a tooth for a tooth." But I say to you, Do not resist an evildoer. But if anyone strikes you on the right check, turn the other also. . .
>
> You have heard that it was said, "You shall love your neighbor and hate your enemy." But I say to you, Love your enemies and pray for those who persecute you. (Matthew 5:38-39, 43-44, NRSV)

Jesus offered encouragement to those who labor for peace. "Blessed are the peacemakers," he said, "for they will be called children of God" (Matthew 5:9, NRSV).

Jesus' resistance to the power of Rome was nonviolent resistance. He allowed himself to be arrested in the garden of Gethsemane.

He rebuked the disciple who cut off the soldier's ear, touched and restored it. When Jesus accepted death on a cross, he rejected violence and military might as a solution to conflict and modeled instead a way of courageous and self-sacrificial obedience to God's way of love, forgiveness, and reconciliation.

In his parting words to his disciples during the Last Supper Jesus told them:

> Peace I leave with you; my peace I give to you. I do not give to you as the world gives. Do not let your hearts be troubled, and do not let them be afraid. (John 14:27, NRSV)

But after Jesus' death on the cross, his followers were discouraged and frightened. They were assembled in a house with locked doors, when the risen Jesus appeared to them. He greeted them with a greeting of peace, identified himself to them by showing his wounds, and then again offered his peace, "Peace be with you. As the Father has sent me, so I send you" (John 20:21, NRSV). With these words he gave the gift of the Holy Spirit.

For Christians, all discussion of peace "must be seen within the context of the unique revelation of God that is Jesus Christ and of the reign of God which Jesus proclaimed and inaugurated."[2] These are the words of the National Conference of Catholic Bishops in their 1983 pastoral letter on war and peace—*The Challenge of Peace: God's Promise and Our Response*. To my way of thinking, this document is an extraordinary gift of American Roman Catholicism to all Christendom and I cannot recommend it highly enough for both personal and group study. The bishops begin by declaring the sacred Scriptures as the foundation for confronting the subject of war and peace and then discuss "peace and the kingdom" in both testaments.

In the New Testament section, their words about Jesus and the community of believers are particularly eloquent:

> As his first gift to his followers, the risen Jesus gave his gift of peace. This gift permeated the meetings between the risen Jesus and his followers (John 20:19-29). So intense was that gift

and so abiding was its power that the remembrance of that gift and the daily living of it became the hallmark of the community of faith. Simultaneously, Jesus gave his spirit to those who followed him. These two personal and communal gifts are inseparable. In the spirit of Jesus the community of believers was enabled to recognize and to proclaim the savior of the world.[3]

Jesus' followers gathered to form the first churches. During the time of the Christian persecution by Roman authorities, believers were comforted and strengthened by the peace of Christ. As he was imprisoned and waiting trial, Paul wrote a letter of encouragement to the Philippians:

Rejoice in the Lord always; again I will say, Rejoice. Let your gentleness be known to everyone. The Lord is near. Do not worry about anything, but in everything by prayer and supplication with thanksgiving let your requests be made known to God. And the peace of God, which surpasses all understanding, will guard your hearts and your minds in Christ Jesus.

(Philippians 4:4-7, NRSV)

As the first believers sought to establish an identity apart from Jews, the roots of conflict and prejudice were born. Not only did Jews not accept Jesus as the Christ, the long-awaited Messiah, but also they were blamed for Jesus' death. Called "Christ killers," over the centuries Jews were marginalized, ghettoized, persecuted. Hitler's attempted genocide—the murder of millions of Jews in the *Shoah*, or Holocaust—had an indelible impact on the psyche of the Jewish people.

From the April day in 1948 when the State of Israel was established by the United Nations, there has been conflict and turmoil in the land. Palestinians call Israeli Independence Day the "Day of Catastrophe." The violence—bombings, bloodshed, death, cycles of retaliation and retribution between Israelis and Palestinians (both Muslim and Christian)—began its seemingly intractable course. Jerusalem, holy to all three faiths, is a city divided.

In an effort to bring a measure of peace and reconciliation between Christian and Jews, Pope John Paul II made a pilgrimage to Jerusalem at the turn of the millennium, in March 2000. The trip had multiple purposes. Not only did he want to apologize for Christian injustices against Judaism, he also wanted to stand in solidarity with Palestinian Christians, to demonstrate the importance of interfaith dialogue, and to satisfy his yearning to visit holy sites.

One evening an interfaith meeting took place at the Notre Dame Center just outside the Old City. It was intended to be a demonstration of cooperation, and the planned climax of the gathering was to be a round of handshaking and the planting of an olive tree.

But the event did not turn out as designed. Things went badly as speakers went off script and gave offense. When one participant abruptly left the stage, it was clear that the tree planting had to go by the wayside. Munib Younan, Lutheran bishop of Jerusalem, was later to ask, "Was this session a fiasco, as the *Jerusalem Post* suggested?" He answered his own question saying: "No, it was a bitter reality. There can be no true dialogue without paying attention to reality."

Bishop Younan had an explanation for what went wrong: "The ground was not fertile for the desired outcome. It had not been well prepared, nor had it been plowed."

He concluded:

The decade of the 1990s in many ways provided a lot of promise for Jewish-Christian-Muslim trialogue. How sad that the new millennium began on such an ominous note. Much progress seemed to be lost, and discussions seemed to be at a standstill. It seemed to be a foreshadowing of more difficult days to come.[4]

Some fundamentalist Christians view the turmoil in the Holy Land as part of God's plan. They see events there as a prelude to the Second Coming foretold in the Book of Revelation. They anticipate that unbelievers will be "left behind" at the appearing, that only born-again Christians will be saved.[5] Quite comfortable about making claims about God's terrifying judgment that will divide families, they cite words of Jesus on the controversial character of his mission:

Do you think that I have come to bring peace to the earth? No, I tell you, but rather division! From now on five in one household will be divided, three against two and two against three; they will be divided:

father against son
        and son against father,
mother against daughter
        and daughter against mother,
mother-in-law against her daughter-in-law
        and daughter-in-law against mother-in-law.

(Luke 12:51-53, NRSV)

There is no doubt that this passage is problematic for Christians who hold a very different view of God's nature.

In his message that night at the Notre Dame Center in Jerusalem, Pope John Paul caused some discomfort when he referred to 1 John 4:20: "If you say you love God and hate your brother, you are a liar."[6]

We also read in 1 John 4:7:

Beloved, let us love one another, because love is from God; everyone who loves is born of God and knows God.   (NRSV)

Everyone who loves knows God. This is the understanding held by many Christians of God's inclusive, extravagant love that embraces humankind. This love is made known by the Prince of Peace and is the way to peace.

When I consider the call to peacemaking, I think of the strenuous effort of parents and teachers to socialize toddlers. They exhort, "Don't hit! Use words!" The instruction seems so elementary. How can our nation justify our preemptive, first strike in Iraq?

Christian writer Anne Lamott wisely observes:

> Hitting first has always been the mark of evil. I don't think one great religious or spiritual thinker has ever said otherwise. Everyone, from almost every tradition, agrees on five things.
>
> Rule 1: We are all family.
> Rule 2: You reap exactly what you sow, that is, you cannot grow tulips from zucchini seeds.
> Rule 3: Try to breathe every few minutes or so.
> Rule 4: It helps beyond words to plant bulbs in the dark of winter.
> Rule 5: It is immoral to hit first.[7]

---

[1] For this discussion I am indebted to Howard E. Galley, *The Ceremonies of the Eucharist.* Cambridge, Massachusetts: Cowley Publications, 1989, p. 97.

[2] Jim Castelli, *The Bishops and the Bomb: Waging Peace in a Nuclear Age.* Garden City, New York: Doubleday & Co., Inc., 1983. This comes from "The Pastoral Letter on War and Peace, The Challenge of Peace: God's Promise and Our Response," pp. 205–206.

[3] Ibid., p. 208.

[4] Munib Younan, *Witnessing for Peace: In Jerusalem and the World.* Minneapolis: Fortress Press, 2003. pp. 158-159.

[5] The best-selling series of novels by Tim LaHaye and Jerry B. Jenkins, beginning with *Left Behind,* is popular with Christians who hold this belief. Please see my discussion of the Left Behind series in Chapter 5.

[6] Munib Younan, p. 159.

[7] Anne Lamott, *Plan B: Further Thoughts on Faith.* New York: Riverhead Books, 2005, pp. 313.

OBSTACLES TO BREAKING CYCLES OF VIOLENCE

*If the most ingrained of inhuman religious prejudice
[anti-Jewish bigotry] can be uprooted, so can other religiously
justified bigotries and barbarities—from male supremacy,
to ethnic chauvinism, to the idolatry of nationalism,
to the complacency of the affluent who mistake their excess
for a divine blessing, to the rage of the dispossessed
who can see suicidal violence as sacred.*

James Carroll[1]

In his last days, as he came near and saw Jerusalem, Jesus wept. The moment that Luke describes was a poignant one. Jesus' heart was heavy as he gazed over the city. "If you, even you, had only recognized on this day the things that make for peace!" (Luke 19:41-42, NRSV). Earlier in the Gospel narrative, Jesus had lamented, "Jerusalem, Jerusalem, the city that kills the prophets and stones those who are sent to it! How often I desired to gather your children together as a hen gathers her brood under her wings, and you were not willing!" (Luke 13:34, NRSV).

Two millennia after the death of Jesus, Jerusalem knows no peace. The ongoing, bloody war between Israelis and Palestinians would make Jesus weep today. If only we recognized "the things that make for peace." An important step toward achieving peace in Jerusalem and in our war-torn world is recognizing the obstacles to peace—the things that make peace so elusive. Insight into why peace has been so difficult to achieve is desperately needed.

My own belief in the living God means that I believe that "God is still speaking." Revelation continues. Through the gift of the Holy Spirit, God reveals God-Self in the unfolding of our days. Pastor

John Robinson articulated this belief when he reminded his followers as they prepared to set sail on the Mayflower in 1620, "The Lord hath yet more light and truth to break forth from his Word."[2]

During the twentieth century, perhaps the most brutal in all human history, new discoveries about human nature and culture were made by social scientists—psychologists, sociologists, anthropologists—that would greatly benefit peace activists of all faith traditions (and none). Many contemporary theologians are integrating this research and learning into their work. It is my strong contention that being knowledgeable about new discoveries can be a great source of help for peacemakers.

While this may seem a reasonable or even obvious statement to most readers, the fact is that for many people the warfare between science and theology has not been resolved. It continues. For example, the teaching of evolution in the schools is a live issue for creationists. For fundamentalists of all persuasions, God's self-revelation was complete long ago. Their struggle is against modernity. The anti-intellectualism in American life that Richard Hofstader described in the early 1960s as a persistent trait in our history is with us still.[3] Sad to say, some politicians are known to manipulate it to their advantage.

For Christians who hold original sin as central and basic, the essential sinfulness of human nature is, of course, *the* problem, *the* obstacle to peace. Violence was introduced into the world when Cain killed his brother, Abel, and so it was and will be. (Interestingly, there is no concept of innate human sinfulness in Islam.)

Christians who hold a different idea of human nature—who see human beings as essentially good, capable of progressing in knowledge and wisdom, and even called to be co-partners with God in the ongoing work of peace and justice—will be more open to the notion that learning has a significant contribution to make to an objective that is within the realm of human possibility. This, I believe, is Chris Hedges's mind-set when he explains that he wrote

War Is a Force That Gives Us Meaning "not to dissuade us from war but to understand it." [4]

My own strong conviction about how valuable deepening knowledge of human nature can be and the difference it can make when integrated with faith, comes from my study of Sigmund Freud's contribution to the practice of ministry. Freud's exploration of the unconscious, and his concepts of repression, projection, transference, etc., gave rise to the movement known as clinical pastoral education (CPE). Today a unit of CPE is required of most seminarians/ divinity students. Because of psychoanalytical discoveries, clergypersons are now far better equipped to be effective pastoral counselors and also to recognize when mental illness is beyond their training to handle. My research into the history of this progressive movement, summarized in *Ministry After Freud*,[5] gives me hope for what behavioral science can bring to conflict resolution, diplomacy, and peace making.

To be fully honest with my readers, I must report the findings of James Hillman, a well-known and well-respected psychologist, a leader in Jungian and post-Jungian thought. He concludes that a terrible love of war is a primary element of the human condition that is not to be changed. He writes that "Ares [or Mars, the god of war] is ever-present; he belongs in the scheme of things."[6] Hillman is extremely critical of Hedges, and says emphatically "love is not an answer to war."[7]

Thus Hedges's educated and deeply felt book on war fails finally because it ends with the usual Christian paean to love:...The retreat to love leaves untouched the important question that each of us as Christians must pose: why is Christianity, which entered the world as a religion of love and has distinguished itself from other world religions by the message of love in its founder and its apostles and exemplified in its martyrs and saints, also so martial? Its notion of love has not converted the god of war, and in fact the Christian culture has inspired the greatest long-lasting war machine of any culture anywhere.[8]

Hillman's *A Terrible Love of War* is not for the faint of soul. As he explains, his chapter "Religion Is War" is an attempt at shock therapy.[9] I recommend this book to all serious students of the psychological origins of war and also to citizens of the U.S. whose notion of patriotism requires them to be willing to be critical of the country they love:

> Hypocrisy in America is not a sin but a necessity and a way of life. It makes possible armories of mass destruction side by side with the proliferation of churches, cults, and charities. Hypocrisy holds the nation together so that it can preach, and practice what it does not preach.[10]

I am more optimistic than James Hillman. My thinking is more in sync with that of Chris Hedges. I am hopeful that cycles of violence may be broken if we can identify them, learn what is at stake, and then act to change our thinking and behaviors. In this section I will focus on four powerful obstacles to breaking cycles of violence: religions' exclusive truth claims, the violence of God in sacred texts and popular culture, state-sponsored violence as a solution to violence, and human violence as giver of meaning.

---

[1] James Carroll, "Muslim, Jew, Christians, and Peace" in *Crusade: Chronicles of an Unjust War*. New York: Metropolitan Books, 2004, p. 82.

[2] In 1853, George Rawson composed a hymn, "We Limit Not the Truth of God," that recalls these words.

[3] Richard Hofstader, *Anti-Intellectualism in American Life*. New York: Alfred A. Knopf, 1963.

[4] Chris Hedges, *War Is a Force That Gives Us Meaning*. New York: Anchor Books, 2003, p. 17.

[5] Allison Stokes, *Ministry After Freud*. New York: Pilgrim Press, 1985. (The book is now out of print; however, I am working on a revised, expanded edition.)

[6] James Hillman, *A Terrible Love of War*. New York: Penguin Books, 2004, p. 202.

[7] Ibid., p. 210.

[8] Ibid., p. 211.

[9] Ibid., p. 199.

[10] Ibid., p. 197.

4

RELIGIONS' EXCLUSIVE
TRUTH CLAIMS

Twelve days after the terrorists attacks of September 11, 2001, a national prayer service was held at Yankee Stadium. Sharing the stage were an imam, a rabbi, a Roman Catholic cardinal, Sikh and Hindu holy men, and a Lutheran pastor, the Reverend David Benke. Benke addressed the assembled as "brothers" and "sisters" and invited people to pray, saying:

> The strength we have is the power of love. And the power of love you have received is from God, for God is love. So take the hand of one next to you now and join me in prayer on this field of dreams turned into God's house of prayer.

For this the Reverend Benke was charged with heresy. Seventeen pastors in the Lutheran Church-Missouri Synod accused him of worshiping publicly in the company of unbelievers. They said that he tolerated *syncretism*—the combining of Christian and non-Christian views—and they called for his dismissal as a clergyman. Despite the fact that Pastor Benke was a prominent leader who presided over the church's Atlantic District of some forty-one thousand baptized believers in the New York region, a church vice president was assigned to investigate the case against him.

The accusations drew headlines, embarrassing the church's national leaders, and causing the synod to issue a letter that barred the parties from discussing the Benke case, to order the church newspaper to stop reporting on it, and to pull references to it from the church's Web site. As *The New York Times* reported:

Other Protestant denominations have long stayed aloof from

interfaith worship. But the charges against Pastor Benke . . . stand out in the aftermath of Sept. 11, when imams and priests, rabbis and preachers stood shoulder to shoulder to pray for the nation.

The incident raised the important question of how a religion can reach out to other faiths while maintaining its own integrity. For the pastors accusing Benke of heresy, the issue is profound. Their sense was that once a faith compromises on one principle, its whole architecture is threatened. A clergyman from Minnesota explained:

> When we're dealing with those who are not Christians—Hindus and Muslims—in those cases, St. Paul talks about not being yoked with unbelievers... It gives the appearance that their God and our God are the same, and they are not, or there are valid other religions, and there are none... Christianity is very exclusive in that Jesus Christ is the savior.

Another clergyman, from Missouri, charged that Pastor Benke took part in idolatry, or the worship of a God not conceived as the God of the Trinity. Another, the publisher of an unofficial Lutheran newspaper, explained:

> We don't hate the Muslims, the Jews, the Sikhs. We love them, therefore we want to let them know they are lost, they are eternally lost, unless they believe in Jesus.[1]

Here we have a clear statement of exclusive Christian truth claims that are a powerful obstacle to breaking the cycle of violence. Whether these claims lead to physical violence and destruction, such claims inflict a kind of spiritual violence. Can one truly "love" persons, while disrespecting their beliefs, while telling them that they are eternally lost *unless...* ? Is love for the Other manifested when one insists that what one believes is the superior—and only—way to believe?

The positive value of the storm over David Benke's invitation to interfaith prayer at Yankee Stadium is that such questions about the exclusivist point of view are being raised and debated. Fortunately, Pastor Benke received full support from members of his congregation. Messages of overwhelming support were also sent to the synod's president, whose response toward the emotional controversy was, "Let charity prevail." It did. For praying hand-in-hand with believers from other religions, the clergyman did not lose his job. In April 2003, the Lutheran Church-Missouri Synod's dispute resolution panel cleared Benke, restoring his church membership to "good standing." The three-member panel found that the pastor's prayer at Yankee Stadium was Christian.[2]

To seek human community under one God in our time means coming to terms with the fact that the monotheistic religions— Judaism, Christianity, and Islam—hold competing visions of truth. Jews, Christians, and Muslims all profess faith in one God, yet make claims based on sacred texts that their particular understanding of God is decisive. Professor Jack Nelson-Pallmeyer explains it this way:

> Jews claim to be God's chosen people, recipients of land, special promises and noble mission. Christians say Jesus fulfilled Hebrew scriptural promises—a claim denied by Jews—that Jesus is the only way to God, and that evangelizing the world is a Christian obligation. Muslims believe they have received the final and definitive word from God. The Qur'an is Allah's divinely inspired corrective to the errors propagated through the texts and conduct of Jews and Christians. It is the religious duty of Muslims to struggle (jihad) against unbelievers in order to establish a world in accord with Allah's intent.[3]

The result is monotheism's legacy of violence—violence justified by religious faith, by God-is-on-our-side thinking.

Christians identify themselves as believers in one God and know very well that Muslims and Jews do as well; therefore, the notion some Christians expressed during the Benke controversy that "their God and our God" is not the same God is a provocative one. It has generated much discussion.

A series entitled "Do Christians and Muslims worship the same God?" appeared in the *Christian Century* in the spring of 2004. The articles by noted professors are enormously helpful in sorting out differences and similarities between Muslim and Christian belief in the God of Abraham. Yale Divinity School's Lamin Sanneh writes:

> Muslims and Christians agree on the great subject that God exists and that God is one. They disagree, however, about the predicates they use of God. Much of the Christian language about God affirms Jesus as God in self-revelation, and much of the Muslim language about God seeks exception to that Christian claim.[4]

This disagreement drew public attention with one outspoken Christian evangelical's declaration—"My God was bigger than his." His words provoked much controversy, pain, anger, and division. They also demonstrated that boasts of religious superiority are an obstacle to human community and peace. What happened?

NBC News broadcast on October 15, 2003, segments of speeches that a top Pentagon official, Army Lt. Gen. William G. Boykin, made at churches in Oklahoma, Oregon, and Florida casting the war on terrorism in religious terms. In speaking about the battle against a Muslim warlord in Somalia, this highly decorated Special Forces combat veteran told an audience of Baptists in Florida in January, "I knew my God was bigger than his. I knew that my God was a real God and his was an idol."[5]

Dressed in uniform and jump boots before a religious group in Oregon in June, the general declared that radical Islamists hated the United States "because we're a Christian nation, because our foundation and our roots are Judeo-Christian… and the enemy is a guy named Satan." He repeatedly told Christian groups and prayer meetings that President George W. Bush was chosen by God to lead the global fight against Satan.

After this story broke, President Bush rebuked General Boykin on several occasions, saying that his opinion "doesn't reflect my point of view or the point of view of this administration." Reporters pointed out that President Bush has made a point of praising Islam as a "religion of peace" and has criticized evangelicals who call Islam a dangerous faith.

The controversy provided a teachable moment for many, including General Boykin himself. In a statement released by the Pentagon, he apologized to those who were offended by his words. He said he did not mean to insult Islam and he was sad his comments created a fury. He sees a battle between good and evil, the evil being the acts of individuals, not the acts of religion.

In response to the my-God-is-bigger-than-your-God news story, Columbia journalism student John Kearney wrote a thoughtful essay, "My God *IS* your God." Kearney mentions a Virginia woman who, like many Americans, believes that Muslims, Christians, and Jews do not all pray to the same God. She says, "Muslims pray to Allah. Allah is not the God of Abraham." He responds:

This woman might be surprised that Christian Arabs use "Allah" for God, as do Arabic-speaking Jews. In Aramaic, the language of Jesus, God is "Allaha," just a syllable away from Allah.

Kearney suggests how the American news media can help make the point that God is one. When journalists write about Muslims, or translate from Arabic, they should translate "Allah" as "God." Kearney reminds people:

"There is no god but God" is the first of Islam's five pillars. It is Muhammad's refutation of polytheism. Yet to today's non-Muslims, the locution "there is no God but Allah" reads as an affront, a declaration that inflammatory Allah trumps the Biblical God. This journalistic rendition distorts the meaning of the Muslim confession of faith.[6]

Mutual respect will not come easily. The Trinity is central to Christianity but Muhammad rejected it as polytheistic. In the Qur'an may be found clear statements rejecting Christian Trinitarian belief:

O People of the Book, exceed not the limits in your religion nor speak anything about Allāh, but the truth. The Messiah,

> Jesus, son of Mary, is only a messenger of Allāh and His word which He communicated to Mary and a mercy from Him. So believe in Allāh and His messengers. And say not, Three. Desist, it is better for you. Allāh is only one God. Far be it from His glory to have a son. To Him belongs whatever is in the heavens and whatever is in the earth. And sufficient is Allāh as having charge of affairs.   (4:171, Qur'an)

Christians living in the United States are less likely to be aware of attitudes of Muslims that are exclusivist than they are aware of attitudes of Christians that are exclusivist. This is because most Christians have little contact with Muslims. Reasons that Muslims have for claiming that Islam supersedes Christianity may come as a surprise to Christians. Murray Titus, Christian missionary, explains the point of view of Muslims he encountered. In his experience Muslims believe that

> as religions go [Islam] is superior to Christianity. It is more up to date, more modern, for it began six centuries later in time. ...As one student of Islam puts it, the Moslem sincerely thinks that Christianity does not offer men and women a religious experience that is higher and better and more perfect than that offered by Islam, but, on the other hand, that it drags them back to a religious stage that for a long time has been a back number. He thinks that we are turning the clock backwards.[7]

This attitude will surely be disconcerting to Christians who are convinced that their own religion is the more enlightened. Given religious differences, what are Christians to do? The apostle Paul wrote a letter to the congregation at Ephesus imploring Christians:

> I therefore, the prisoner in the Lord, beg you to lead a life worthy of the calling to which you have been called, with all humility and gentleness, with patience, bearing with one another in love, making every effort to maintain the unity of the Spirit in the bond of peace.   (Ephesians 4:1-3, NRSV)

Are Christians to bear *only* with one another in love, or is their loving to extend to all people? When Christians claim that only Christians can be saved, do they jeopardize faithful efforts to forge bonds of peace? Do they undermine hope for achieving a sense of human unity, interdependence, and the common good?

Fortunately, we are beginning to reflect, talk, and learn more about the competing and exclusive truth claims that have divided and still divide us, claims that have generated and continue to generate violence.[8] If the global village we now inhabit encourages us to examine the need to feel our faith is superior, and leads us to be more open to the spiritual experience of people of other religions, we will have made progress toward peace.

---

[1] Daniel J. Wakin, "Seeing Heresy in a Service for Sept. 11," *The New York Times*, February 8, 2002, p. B1.

[2] *The New York Times*, May 13, 2003, p. B11.

[3] Jack Nelson-Pallmeyer, *Is Religion Killing Us? Violence in the Bible and the Quran*. New York: Trinity Press International, 2003, p. 33.

[4] Lamin Sanneh, "Do Christians and Muslims worship the same God?" *The Christian Century*, May 4, 2004, p. 35.

[5] "General Casts War in Religious Terms," *Los Angeles Times*, October 15, 2003.

[6] John Kearney, "My God IS Your God," *The New York Times*, January 28, 2004.

[7] Murray T. Titus, *The Young Moslem Looks at Life*. New York: Friendship Press, 1937, p. 129. (See mention of Titus in Chapter 3.)

[8] As this book goes to press, I have learned of an important, new collection of essays, *War Or Words? Interreligious Dialogue as an Instrument of Peace*, Donald W. Musser and C. Dixon Sutherland, eds. (Cleveland: The Pilgrim Press, 2005). In this, Charles A. Kimball writes about "Absolute Truth Claims: Blockade to Dialogue."

5

THE VIOLENCE OF GOD IN SACRED
TEXTS AND POPULAR CULTURE

A story of the Hebrew people in Babylonian Exile is told in Psalm 137. Far from their own country, they sit by the rivers of Babylon and weep. They are remembering home, remembering Jerusalem's fall. They set Jerusalem as their highest joy and tell themselves they will never forget. Seeking amusement, their captors torment them by asking them to sing songs of Zion. But the Hebrew people refuse. They hang up their lyres on the poplar trees—"How shall we sing the Lord's song in a foreign land?" (Psalm 137:4, RSV). The question expresses the anguish of exiles and refugees everywhere and in all time who have longed for home. The poignancy of the words stirs my heart and I commit them to memory: "How shall we sing the Lord's song in a foreign land?"

And then the Psalm takes me to a place I do not want to go. It closes with shocking sentiments. The Revised Standard Version (RSV), verses 8-9, reads:

O daughter of Babylon, you devastator!
Happy shall be he who requites you
    with what you have done to us!
Happy shall he be who takes your little ones
    and dashes them against the rock!

The English translation in the Tanakh (JPS) is slightly different:
Fair Babylon, you predator,
    a blessing on him who repays you in kind
    what you have inflicted on us;
    a blessing on him who seizes your babies
    and dashes them against the rocks!

The will to murder little ones, innocent babies, out of a human desire for revenge is repugnant, but even more so, the invocation of God's blessing. Horrific images of events in Beslan, Russia, in September 2004 come to mind—the violent deaths of hundreds of children seized as hostages by Chechen terrorists on the opening day of school.

In using Psalm 137 in a liturgical service, I stop short of those repulsive closing words. I refuse to repeat them or to ask others to do so. And so begins the process of consciousness raising—of noticing, reflecting upon, and critiquing violence in both testaments. Instances of human violence in the name of God are recorded there. Also recorded are human experiences of God as violent and terrifying.

Jack Nelson-Pallmeyer has studied violence in the Bible and the Qur'an. An assistant professor of justice and peace studies at the University of St. Thomas in St. Paul, Minnesota, he concludes that an essential act of faithfulness for believers in the twenty-first century is challenging our texts and our traditions. This proposal will be provocative for many in the Abrahamic faiths.

In his book *Is Religion Killing Us?* Nelson-Pallmeyer argues that the dominant themes of "sacred" texts are portrayals of God as punishing and violent and of God's power as coercive and abusive. The problem is not that people take passages out of context and twist them in order to justify violence, that they misinterpret the text; rather, the problem is that religiously justified violence is embedded in "sacred" texts. In other words, his fundamental claim is that *actual* violence is at the heart of the Bible and the Qur'an. "This is the elephant in the room of which nobody speaks."[1]

A student of the relation of religion, violence, and peace, Nelson-Pallmeyer does not deny that the Hebrew Scriptures, the Christian New Testament, and the Qur'an contain stories urging compassionate living, social justice, and ethical conduct. Nevertheless, he writes,

> The collective weight of all passages in these texts that advocate
> ethical behavior or present evidence of a loving, compassionate

God cannot, however, overcome the violent images and expectations of God that overwhelm these "sacred" texts. God's violence or human violence justified in service to God is sometimes understood to be the principal means to justice in, or at the end of, history. At other times, ethical conduct is urged under the threat of God's punishing violence. God's violence is at times so pervasive, unpredictable, vindictive, or destructive that it reflects a deep and troubling pathology. In such cases, we can say that if human beings acted as God does or as God tells them to act, then they would rightfully be considered certifiably insane.[2]

What is the evidence? I cannot in a few pages try to review arguments that Nelson-Pallmeyer takes a book to develop. I am reluctant to discuss his charges of God's violence in the Hebrew Scriptures (in the Exodus, Exile, and apocalyptic images). And I am particularly reluctant to discuss his charges of God's violence in the Qur'an (threats of hell, promises of paradise, God as Holy Warrior). These are sensitive subjects that deserve careful and extended treatment by scholars in these faith traditions. I will, however, speak to his Violence-of-God critique in the New Testament, particularly as it relates to the cross. Professor Nelson-Pallmeyer writes that many Christians believe that a gracious God so loved the world that he sent his only Son "to die in our place so that we might avoid our deserved punishment, go to heaven instead of hell, and have eternal life." He says that brutal images of God remain hidden behind these interpretations:

If we believe that Jesus died for us so that we will not be condemned, then we should ask, "Condemned by whom?" The answer is, God. What remains unstated in classic Christian statements of faith is that Jesus dies in order to save us from God, not from sin. More precisely, Jesus' sacrificial death saves us from a violent God who punishes sin.[3]

What Nelson-Pallmeyer describes here, of course, is the theology of the Atonement. He notes, "The scapegoat ritual of the Day of Atonement, known as Yom Kippur, became a prominent frame of reference for sacrificial interpretations of Jesus' death."[4] Such interpretations are predominant in the world of Christendom today. Believers thank and praise Jesus for shedding his blood to redeem them from their personal sin. Jesus was the sacrificial Lamb of God who died to save them. Some Christians interpret the meaning of Jesus' death on the cross differently. They believe that God is a life-giving God, not a death-dealing God. God did not require Jesus' death. Jesus died on a cross at the hands of those who could not abide his way of radical love, of nonviolence, and justice seeking. With perfect integrity, courage, and trust in God, the Creator and Life-Giver, Jesus set his face toward Jerusalem and never turned back. He rejected worldly power and the warring ways of the world. He taught love of enemy. The consequence was his death. God suffered with Jesus on the cross, but did not intervene. God's response to human death-dealing was the Resurrection.

In speaking of the meaning of the cross and traditional atonement theology, some suggest taking the word *atonement* and pronouncing it with a different emphasis: "at/one/ment." Jesus' own will was *at one* with the will of God. Jesus followed in God's way of love perfectly. He taught us to "pray for those who persecute you." He showed the world the life-giving way to peace.

James Carroll, author of *Crusade: Chronicles of an Unjust War* and lecturer on Jewish-Christian-Muslim reconciliation, makes a direct connection between the Crusades and the theology of the Atonement. Carroll points out that the Crusades were "the first time that violence was defined by the church as a sacred act. 'God wills it!' was the battle cry with which Pope Urban II launched the First Crusade in 1095."[5] Several years later, in 1098, that campaign of political violence was given its justification by Saint Anselm, who promulgated the interpretation of the cross that became "atonement" theology. Carroll writes:

> In this understanding, God became a man, in the person of Jesus, not to preach a message of love, nor to reveal the good-

46

ness of creation, nor even to offer hope through resurrection—but expressly to die a brutal death on the cross. Jesus underwent the blood-soaked fate of the scapegoat. In this theology, it was the violence of Golgotha that saved humankind—an idea that soon became enshrined in a Christian religious imagination fixated on the crucifix.[6]

A Roman Catholic, James Carroll explains that Vatican II decisively moved away from Anselm's atonement schema and "the oedipal antagonism that sets father against son in mortal conflict." Vatican II deemphasized Good Friday in favor of Easter Sunday and thus put the Resurrection back at the center of the faith. The focus of faith is the "real passions" of Christ— "for truth, for love, and for life."[7]

Given Carroll's appreciation of the reforms of the Second Vatican Council, the reader can imagine what he has to say about Mel Gibson's violent film *The Passion of the Christ.* Carroll sees it as an obscene movie. The brutal scene of the flogging of Jesus approaches the pornographic. At bottom, Carroll views "Gibson's violence fantasies" as "a fantasy of infinite male toughness." There is no resurrection in the film. It is "a triumph of sadomasochistic exploitation,"[8] according to Carroll. What is more, it is dangerous because it resuscitates the old "Christ Killer" charge against the Jews.

James Carroll draws a connection between the Crusades, atonement theology, Gibson's film, and what he calls George W. Bush's crusade against terrorism. The journalist draws on his remarkable knowledge of history, theology, the church, contemporary affairs, and popular culture to offer a moral vision that is deeply compelling to me. I especially appreciate his critique of the Iraqi war:

The only way "this crusade, this war on terrorism," in the president's phrase, will not be a replay of past crimes and tragedies is if we repudiate not just the word *crusade* but the mind of the crusader. We can start by acknowledging above all, that when humans go to war, God in no way wills it.[9]

In his Acknowledgments in *Crusade,* James Carroll writes, "I have dedicated this book, in love, to William Sloane Coffin, Jr., who taught me the first lessons of peace." When I read this, I was not the least surprised because much of what Carroll writes is reminiscent of his mentor. Bill Coffin has spoken and preached passionately against the Iraq war—indeed, against the Cold War, the Vietnam War, and against nuclear arms. He is a prophet in our time. Chaplain at Yale during the Civil Rights marches and Vietnam War protests, head of SaneFreeze during nuclear disarmament negotiations, and senior minister at the Riverside Church in Manhattan during the Gulf War, Bill Coffin has witnessed to the good news of God's love with a clarity, eloquence, and power that is unrivaled, as far as I am concerned. He inspires me to put my faith into action.

For those who would study the relationship between sacred texts of terror, religious violence, and war, the popular response to *The Passion of the Christ* is a significant phenomenon in American culture. Another significant phenomenon that deserves attention is the popular response to the apocalyptic Left Behind novels. At the time I write, over sixty-two million copies have been sold. They are outselling Stephen King, John Grisham, and every other pop novelist in America.[10]

When in the fall of 2001, I overheard students in a prayer group talking about how they couldn't wait for *Desecration* to arrive in the bookstores, I was clueless. When I inquired, I was told that *Desecration* was the latest sequel in a series of best-sellers written by Tim LaHaye and Jerry B. Jenkins. Normally pretty well informed, I felt totally out of it. How had I been unaware of such a big development? I finally realized that despite my desire to promote diversity, I had never heard of the Left Behind novels because of the distance between conservative Christians and me.

I decided it was time to catch up on what they were reading. Little did I realize what an education this would be and how disturbed I would become by what I learned. Before long I was writing to friends to sound the alarm: there was a world of apocalyptic Christian thought out there that they were oblivious of (as I had been), and they needed to look into it.

As it turns out, I was not the only one who hadn't noticed. It took some time for the media to discover that one in eight Americans are reading these books. (Statistics from the publisher, Tyndale House, show that 71 percent of the readers are from the South and Midwest, and just 6 percent from the Northeast.[11])

These works are not sacred texts, of course, but fiction. One student, a big fan of the novels, dismissed critical questions I tried to raise, saying they are just "fun," "entertaining," and not to be taken seriously. I cannot accept her dismissal of my concern, given that millions of people are being influenced by this thought world and that the authors claim the series is biblically based.

The Book of Revelation, the last book of the New Testament, is the reference point.

Left Behind, the first novel of the series, opens with the "Rapture." In one cataclysmic instant, millions of people disappear. Christ has come in the air to claim his own, and all other human beings are left behind. Worldwide chaos ensues and the Tribulation begins, the seven years when people are given a second chance to come to faith before the Apocalypse. Four protagonists representing those left behind during the vanishings—Rayford Steele, his daughter Chloe, Pastor Bruce Barnes, and news writer Buck Williams—make a decision for Christ and form the Tribulation Force to challenge the murderous forces of evil that have been unleashed.

Their opponent is Nicolae Carpathia, the Antichrist. (The third book in the series is *Nicolae.*) Promising to unite the devastated globe in one peaceful village, this power-hungry, charismatic man becomes secretary-general of the United Nations. Leaders of the major religions happen to be in New York when he arrives at the U.N. to begin his takeover. He urges them "to come together, to agree on some all-inclusive effort at tolerance that would respect their shared beliefs." Please note that a tactic of the Antichrist is using the United Nations as a setting and advocating an "all-inclusive" effort at "tolerance." Note also that when Nicolae Carpathia plans to disarm the world, it is "the American militia movement"[12] that opposes him and those prepared to initiate action against him before it is too late are Egypt, England, and "patriotic militia forces in the U.S."[13]

The four protagonists are locked in a deadly struggle against Nicolae in the twelve books *Newsweek* calls "Biblical techno-thrillers":

> It's old-time religion with a sci-fi sensibility: the Tribulation timetable comes from LaHaye; the cell phones, Land Rovers— and characters struggling with belief and unbelief—come from Jenkins.[14]

The Left Behind message seems calculated to induce fear. One must accept Jesus Christ as Lord and Savior now, before it's too late, or suffer the hideous consequences—of being left behind, of being separated from faithful loved ones who are saved (parents, husbands, wives, children), and of facing the horror of the end. Being a Christian is not sufficient protection from this hideous fate, for one might be attending church only perfunctorily, or one might be attending a "dead church." One must be passionate in one's faith, not lukewarm, but deeply committed, born-again. The end— making a decision for Christ—justifies the means—manipulating people's deepest insecurities and fears.

I read these books with a red pen in hand, underlining the many passages that in my estimation could do psychological or spiritual harm. What I find so dangerous is the confusing mix of small doses of sound theology with large doses of unsound theology, the gospel message with dire threats of apocalyptic punishment, Christian faith with James Bond-like, thriller fiction.

Randomly I open the second book in the series, *Tribulation Force*, and come upon a passage I have starred. It's about Pastor Bruce Barnes, one of the Tribulation Force team. He is preaching:

Bruce told his own story yet again, how he had lived a phony life of pietism and churchianity for years, and how when God came to call, he had been found wanting and had been left behind, without his wife and precious children.

Bruce witnesses to his new faith, saying that he never wants to stop telling what Christ has done for him. The Bible says that the cross offends, so that if his listeners are offended, he is doing his job. Bruce continues:

We've already missed the Rapture, and now we live in what will soon become the most perilous period of history. Evangelists used to warn parishioners that they could be struck by a car or die in a fire and thus they should not put off coming to Christ. I'm telling you that should you be struck by a car or caught in a fire, it may be the most merciful way you can die. Be ready this time.[15]

Throughout the books is the theme, "Israel remains largely unbelieving and soon will suffer for it!" Unless Jews are converted, they are lost.[16]

After reading the first two books in the series, as well as *The Vanishings: Left Behind, The Kids* (an edition of the first book reworked for teenagers), I quit reading. I was too distressed to continue. Particularly upsetting was the young people's edition, about four kids left behind to "face the earth's last days together." The adult characters are the same, so we again encounter Pastor Bruce Barnes. Here is the book's conclusion:

For now they were simply four kids from the same town who shared a common horror and grief. Bruce seemed to have in mind for them a future as a small group. That sounded good to each, especially in their gnawing loneliness.

When the video ended, each sat stunned that the pastor had known in advance all that was now taking place. Clearly this was truth. Certainly this demanded their attention and a decision. Each sat staring as Bruce posed the question of the ages.

"Are you ready?" he said. "Will you receive Christ?"[17]

To me, playing on the abandonment fear that every child has in order to win him or her to Christ is reprehensible. WWJD? What would Jesus do? What would Jesus have to say about *The Vanishings*, which Jerry B. Jenkins and Tim LaHaye dedicate "to our own kids"?

Now lest the reader think I am being unduly concerned, I point out that I am not alone in taking offense. When the last book in the series, *Glorious Appearing*, was published, Nicholas Kristof of *The New York Times* wrote an Op-Ed piece about it.[18] He did so because "this matters in the real world, in the same way that fundamentalist Islamic tracts in Saudi Arabia do." *In Glorious Appearing* Jesus returns to Earth to wipe out all non-Christians from the planet, to gather non-Christians to his left and toss them into the fire. Kristof begins by quoting from the book:

Jesus merely raised one hand a few inches and a yawning chasm opened in the earth, stretching far and wide enough to swallow all of them. They tumbled in, howling and screeching, but their wailing was soon quashed and all was silent when the earth closed itself again.

As Kristof retells it:

Jesus merely speaks and the bodies of the enemy are ripped open. Christians have to drive carefully to avoid "hitting splayed and filleted bodies of men and women and horses."

The riders not thrown [the novel continues] leaped from their horses and tried to control them with the reins, but even as they struggled, their own flesh dissolved, their eyes melted and their tongues disintegrated....Seconds later the same plague afflicted the horses, their flesh and eyes and tongues melting away, leaving grotesque skeletons standing, before they, too, rattled to the pavement.

To this Kristof makes the wry comment, "One might have thought that Jesus would be more of an animal lover." I find this quite funny, but what he is writing about here is not funny at all.

The columnist rightly observes:

> If a Muslim were to write an Islamic version of "*Glorious Appearing*" and publish it in Saudi Arabia, jubilantly describing a massacre of millions of non-Muslims by God, we would have a fit.

Kristof draws a connection with the American imprisonment of thousands of Muslims here and abroad after 9/11 and also the torture of prisoners at Abu Ghraib. "It's harder to feel empathy for such people if we regard them as infidels and expect Jesus to dissolve their tongues and eyes any day now."

Kristof admits he has reservations about writing this column. He does not want to mock anyone's religious beliefs and he knows that millions of American readers do believe that the *Glorious Appearing* describes God's will. Ultimately, however, he feels a responsibility to protest intolerance at home. He asks, "Should we really give intolerance a pass if it is rooted in religious faith?" His column, "Jesus and Jihad," answers with a resounding, NO. Kristof concludes:

> People have the right to believe in a racist God, or a God who throws millions of nonevangelicals into hell. I don't think we should ban books that say that. But we should be embarrassed when our best-selling books gleefully celebrate religious intolerance and violence against infidels.
>
> That's not what America stands for, and I doubt that it's what God stands for.

To this I want to add an "Amen!" Tim LaHaye is co-founder of the Moral Majority and the extremist right-wing political intention of the Left Behind series seems clear to me. It's a will to power, to Christian world dominance, very much in the imperial mind-set I discuss in the next chapter.

I conclude by quoting a man whose project is showing how discontinuous much of today's Christianity is with the teachings of Jesus. Bruce Bawer reminds us:

The real Jesus—the Jesus who was incontrovertibly human, even as he was connected to God in a remarkable way that utterly transformed the lives of the people who knew him— was not about asserting power, judging, or destroying; he was about love.... Lose Jesus as a human being and you lose that: You lose Jesus as a model of how to lead a human life; you lose the possibility of love as a guiding principle of human relations; you lose Christianity—or, at least you lose any Christianity worth the name.[19]

Bawer's book, *Stealing Jesus: How Fundamentalism Betrays Christianity*, is an indispensable resource for those who would learn more about why some Christians became so extreme in twentieth-century America. Bawer believes that such Christianity endangers "the stability, democracy, and pluralism not only of the United States but also of the world."[20]

---

[1] Jack Nelson-Pallmeyer, *Is Religion Killing Us?* New York: Trinity Press International, 2003, p. xiv.

[2] Ibid., p. 93.

[3] Ibid., p. 60.

[4] Ibid., p. 61.

[5] James Carroll, *Crusade: Chronicles of an Unjust War.* New York: Metropolitan Books, 2004, p. 24.

[6] Ibid., p. 277.

[7] Ibid., p. 268.

[8] Ibid., p. 273.

[9] Ibid., p. 26.

[10] David Gates, "The Pop Prophets." *Newsweek*, May 24, 2004, p. 46.

[11] Ibid.

[12] Tim LaHaye and Jerry B. Jenkins, *Tribulation Force.* Wheaton, Illinois: Tyndale House Publishers, 1996, p. 127.

[13] Ibid., p. 424.

[14] "The Pop Prophets," p. 46.

[15] *Tribulation Force*, pp. 62–63.

[16] Ibid., p. 402.

[17] Tim LaHaye and Jerry B. Jenkins, *The Vanishings: Left Behind: The Kids*. Wheaton, Illinois: Tyndale House Publishers, Inc., 1998, pp. 145–146.

[18] "Jesus and Jihad." *The New York Times*, Saturday, July 17, 2004, p. A13. The following quotations are all from this column.

[19] Bruce Bawer, *Stealing Jesus: How Fundamentalism Betrays Christianity*. New York: Three Rivers Press, 1997, p. 326.

[20] Ibid., p. 15.

6

STATE-SPONSORED VIOLENCE AS A SOLUTION TO VIOLENCE

Violence by the state, used in response to violence, is another obstacle to peace. That is to say, war is not the answer. The truth of this statement seems so obvious; and yet most believers, people of faith, accept state-sponsored violence as a practical necessity. We look at global conflicts, history, and the human condition, and conclude that world peace is an unrealistic, unachievable goal. We observe that alternatives to military intervention—diplomacy, political action, judicial and police processes, and nonviolent resistance—don't always work. And so we buy into the concept of "just" and "unjust wars."

With Saint Thomas Aquinas at the forefront, religious leaders over time have worked out rules or principles of engagement to justify violence engaged by the state.

The very first principle is: *A just war can only be waged as a last resort. All nonviolent options must be exhausted before the use of force can be justified.*

Another principle is: *A just war can only be fought to redress a wrong suffered.*

As helpful as these principles once may have been, and in conventional warfare still may be, in an era of nuclear war capability, old ideas fall apart. When a nuclear war can destroy all life on the planet, Just War Theory is irrelevant.

"The United States, as the world knows, will never start a war." These words of President John F. Kennedy were spoken in 1963 during the Cold War.[1] At that time the foreign policies of the U.S. and the U.S.S.R. were governed by a military defense strategy known as "MAD"— Mutually Assured Destruction. A balance of nuclear power between the two superpowers would mean that in the event of war, destruction would be mutually assured; therefore, neither power would dare to risk beginning a war. As Kennedy said, and Americans truly believed, the world could be confident that the U.S. would never start a war. If there were to be one, the U.S.S.R. would begin it—as nearly happened when Soviet missiles were sent to Cuba. We came to the brink with the Cuban Missile Crisis.

With the fall of the Berlin Wall and the break-up of the Soviet Union in 1989, the U.S. is now the only superpower. After terrorist attacks on the World Trade Center and the Pentagon, symbols of U.S. economic and military might, President George W. Bush declared a "War on Terrorism." The United States then did what John F. Kennedy had said the United States would never do—we launched a preemptive first strike.

In March 2003, our government started a war in Iraq, a war viewed the world over and named by U.N. Secretary-General Kofi Annan, as unjust and illegal. The Bush administration justified its first strike (calculated to produce "shock and awe") by claiming that Saddam Hussein was collaborating with Osama bin Laden, mastermind of the 9/11 attacks, and that Iraq had weapons of mass destruction (WMD) that Hussein was preparing to use. According to the Bush-appointed 9/11 Commission, both claims proved to be false.

Even when no weapons of mass destruction were found and it was clear that Iraq had posed no imminent threat to the security of the United States, President Bush was not willing to admit that the preemptive strike against Iraqi had been a mistake. And when the fighting, death, devastation, and chaos in Iraq intensified, the administration insisted the world was safer. To admit mistakes, the president contended, would be to show weakness, to confuse the enemy, to send "the wrong signal." To admit mistakes would be to dishonor those who had died defending the country.

The outpouring of sympathy engendered by 9/11 changed to outrage when the U.S. went against the counsel of its allies (with the exception of Great Britain), became the aggressor, and then an occupying force. Before the war began, on February 15, 2003, fifteen million people around the globe had demonstrated against war and for peace. It was the largest worldwide demonstration ever. But blatant disregard of world opinion and "Bring 'em on" bravado after the war began served to isolate the nation.[2]

The revelation of American abuse of prisoners at Abu Ghraib—gross human rights violations—and the president's refusal to hold his secretary of defense (or anyone in senior authority) accountable made matters worse. Given the hatred and animosity engendered by U.S. actions, the inescapable conclusion is that the homeland is now more vulnerable to the threat of terrorism than before 9/11.

Countless American citizens from both political parties became deeply worried by government actions and policies that evidenced a clear departure from America's commitment to the rule of law and human rights.

Reports of torture of prisoners led three Republican Senators—John McCain, John Warner, and Lindsey Graham—to work for legislation that would expressly prohibit cruel, inhumane, or degrading treatment of detainees in U.S. custody. When a fellow senator spoke against the legislation saying that the detainees are not prisoners of war, but terrorists, Senator McCain argued that the debate "is not about who they are. It's about who we are."[3] More than a dozen retired officers—generals, admirals, and former prisoners of war—agreed. They wrote Senator McCain a letter offering support:

> The abuse of prisoners hurts America's cause in the war on terror, endangers U.S. service members who might be captured by the enemy, and is anathema to the values Americans have held dear for generations.

One signer of the letter, John Hutson, a former admiral, told a columnist that if the United States "fails to get its act together with regard to the humane treatment of detainees...we will 'have changed the DNA of what it means to be an American.'"[4]

The escalating militarization of U.S. society has changed our budget priorities from education, health care, and safe communities to huge outlays to military-industrial companies for advanced weapons. Fear is engendered by a constant series of threats—real, created, and imagined. The American people live in a state of alert and anxiety. War is promoted as the means to justice and peace. Nation-building is replacing diplomacy with little or no cohesive international resistance. The U.S. is increasingly behaving as an empire intent on ruling the world, and the words *empire* and *imperial* have come frequently to be used to describe the changing national ethos.[5]

Do we as Americans have the capacity to be self-critical? Are we able to look at the log in our own eye before focusing on the speck in the eye of our neighbor (Matthew 7: 3-5; Luke 6:41-42)? I think the peace of the world depends upon it.

Using violence as a response to violence is not the way. The challenge now is to join with many nations to oppose terrorism not by military might, but by sharing resources and power, practicing respect and engendered hope. The task, too, is to prosecute through international law and police and judicial processes those who continue to use violence.

Jonathan Schell chronicles a history of movements for nonviolent change in his book *The Unconquerable World: Power, Nonviolence, and the Will of the People*.[6] While we usually study history as a chronology of wars, he gives instead a history of successes in nonviolence. Persistent and nonviolent struggles have led to peaceful revolutions in India, South Africa, Czechoslovakia, South Korea, the Philippines, the U.S. (the Civil Rights movement), and other places. Although individuals have often paid a heavy price in blood under violent assault and imprisonment, they have brought about change without war.

What if we were to focus our attention upon the human potential for peace? What if we were to educate ourselves about cultures of peace?—"the hidden side of history," to use of words of Elise

Boulding, former secretary-general of the International Peace Research Association. Dr. Boulding counsels, "We cannot achieve what we cannot imagine."[7]

---

[1] "The Strategy of Peace," *"Let the Word Go Forth": The Speeches, Statements, and Writings of John F. Kennedy, 1947–1963*, Theodore C. Sorensen, ed. New York: Delacorte Press, 1988, p. 290.

[2] On July 2, 2003 President Bush declared that U.S. troops under fire in Iraq were not about to pull out, and he taunted those tempted to attack American forces saying, "Bring 'em on." *www.usatoday.com/new/world/iraq*

[3] Bob Herbert, "Who We Are," *The New York Times*, August 1, 2005, p. A17.

[4] Ibid.

[5] In 2004, there was an outpouring of books with titles that reveal the authors' dismay, apprehension, and sense of alarm about the state of the union. In no particular order, I like just some of them:
- *The Sorrows of Empire: Militarism, Secrecy, and the End of the Republic (The American Empire Project)* by Chalmers Johnson
- *Colossus: The Price of America's Empire* by Niall Ferguson
- *Democracy Matters: Winning the Fight Against Imperialism* by Cornell West
- *Resurrecting Empire: Western Footprints and America's Perilous Path in the Middle East* by Rashid Khalidi
- *Imperial Hubris: Why the West Is Losing the War on Terror* by Anonymous (Michael Scheuer)
- *Hegemony or Survival: America's Quest for Global Dominance* (The American Empire Project) by Noam Chomsky
- *American Dynasty: Aristocracy, Fortune, and the Politics of Deceit in the House of Bush* by Kevin Phillips
- *Imperial Overstretch: George W. Bush and the Hubris of Empire* by Roger Burbach, Jim Tarbell
- *Superpower Syndrome: America's Apocalyptic Confrontation with the World* by Robert Jay Lifton
- *Imperial America: Reflections on the United States of Amnesia* by Gore Vidal
- *Imperial America: The Bush Assault on the World Order* by John Newhouse
- *Empire & Imperialism: A Critical Reading of Michael Hardt and Antonio Negri* by Michael Hardt, Antonio Negri
- *An Ordinary Person's Guide to Empire* by Arundhati Roy

[6] Jonathan Schell, *The Unconquerable World: Power, Nonviolence, and the Will of the People*. New York: Metropolitan Books, 2003.

[7] Elise Boulding, *Cultures of Peace: The Hidden Side of History*. Syracuse, New York: Syracuse University Press, 2000, p. 7.

7

HUMAN VIOLENCE
AS GIVER OF MEANING

A man near and dear to my heart, a Vietnam veteran, was working on a book about his war experience. He called the manuscript "Baptism," which seemed strange to me; but we never talked about the title, or why he chose it. This in itself was probably strange, given my profession and how close we were.

When *Baptism: A Vietnam Memoir* was published in 1999 and I read it, I finally understood that the title was ironic. In this war story (now in its seventh printing), Lawrence Gwin describes his baptism into Evil. As the jacket of the book says, "Through the stench of death and the acrid smell of napalm, he chronicles the Vietnam War in all its nightmarish horror." Fighting against enemy troops in the Ia Drang Valley in some of the war's most horrific battles, Alpha Company of the 1st Cavalry Division sustained incredible losses— 70 percent casualties.

Years after his return from Vietnam, Larry discovered that he suffered from "PTSD"— Post Traumatic Stress Disorder. I well remember that the diagnosis was a welcome one in that it brought him an enormous sense of relief. He could finally give debilitating symptoms a name, and by identifying what was wrong, he could begin the road to healing.

My friend Larry is a remarkable man—a practicing lawyer, a talented writer, a husband and devoted father of two sons, a graduate of Yale's class of 1963, and a member of Skull and Bones. (I am not supposed to reveal—or even know—this, but if the world can know it about George W. Bush and John Kerry, I feel free.) He is also a guy who has experienced hell on earth. When I think about "war as a force that gives meaning," as war correspondent Chris Hedges describes it, I think of Larry as a young man.

In the early pages of his book, Larry explains why he voluntarily enlisted for military service. As an ROTC lieutenant at Yale, he was following in the footsteps of family males. It was an honorable tradition. His first childhood recollection is of the day his father came home from war. Larry vaguely remembers a parade in Washington on VJ Day with flags flying and people dancing in the street. He reflects:

> Perhaps I was destined to serve my country—certainly encouraged by John F. Kennedy's charismatic leadership. Signing up was just another step on the road. After all, we are who we are.
>
> And all the Gwin men had gone. My great-great-grandfather, James Gwin, had joined Davy Crocket and his cronies as they traipsed through Tennessee on their way to fight Mexicans in Texas. James died at the Alamo, leaving a widow and two sons back on their hardscrabble farm. One of those sons, Sylvester, grew up to serve the Confederacy. He lost half of his jaw fighting for John Bell Hood at Franklin, but survived. His manservant, a full-blooded Choctaw, dragged him from the battlefield and cleaned his wound with maggots, and Sylvester went on to farm cotton and raise four sons. One of them, my grandfather Sam, signed on with the Mississippi Volunteers when the Spanish American War broke out. Though he never got close to the action, he bore the moniker "Cap'n" 'til he died.[1]

Being prepared to fight in battle, going off to war, advancing in rank, and earning medals are associated with passage into manhood and manly valor (despite the fact that women are now soldiers, too). As evidence of this, recall the bitter accusations during the presidential election campaign of 2004 around the service records of George W. Bush and John F. Kerry. President Bush was criticized for avoiding military service in Vietnam by going into the National Guard in Texas and of being absent without leave.

Although his opponent was a decorated war veteran, when in television spots the "Swift Boat Veterans" questioned Kerry's entitlement to the medals he had won in Vietnam, Senator John McCain was furious. He said he found the television advertisements "completely nauseating":

If they question Kerry's medals, they question everybody's medals. All those men who found it so hard to come home, who found so little gratitude for their sacrifices when they got here, are going to feel mistreated again. The families of the people whose names are on the monument in Washington will feel wronged, too. The painful wounds we all worked so hard to close will all be reopened.

We've got to get that garbage off the air as soon as we can.[2]

Kerry's service was undermined by the suspicion that he exaggerated his war wounds and his heroism. Bush's service was undermined by his class privilege and avoidance of war. Each positioned himself as the man most capable of leading the country as commander in chief of the armed services.

Chris Hedges is a journalist who has worked in various war zones over almost twenty years—surviving ambush, beating, imprisonment. He has a perspective influenced both by his global experience and by his studies at the Harvard Divinity School. In *War Is a Force That Gives Us Meaning* he writes:

War is a god, as the ancient Greeks and Romans knew, and its worship demands human sacrifice. We urge young men to war, making the slaughter they are asked to carry out a rite of passage. And this rite has changed little over the centuries, centuries in which there has almost continuously been a war raging somewhere on the planet.[3]

Hedges observes:

The enduring attraction of war is this: Even with its destruction and carnage it can give us what we long for in life. It can give us purpose, meaning, a reason for living.[4]

Hedges knows that war is "an enticing elixir," that the rush of battle can be a potent addiction. War is a drug, one that he himself ingested for many years:

> It is peddled by mythmakers—historians, war correspondents, filmmakers, novelists, and the state—all of whom endow it with qualities it often does possess: excitement, exoticism, power, chances to rise above our small stations in life, and a bizarre and fantastic universe that has a grotesque and dark beauty.[5]

Hedges describes not only the *drug* of war, but also the *myth* of war. The myth of war is essential to justify the horrible sacrifices that war requires, he says. It gives justification to human cruelty and stupidity:

> In mythic war we fight absolutes. We must vanquish darkness. It is imperative and inevitable for civilization, for the free world, that good triumph.[6]

But experience of combat dispels the myth of war as the soldier moves from "the abstract to the real," from the "mythic to the sensory."

> The lofty words that inspire people to war—duty, honor, glory—swiftly become repugnant and hollow. They are replaced by the hard, specific images of war, by the prosaic names of villages and roads. The abstract rhetoric of patriotism is obliterated, exposed as the empty handmaiden of myth.[7]

Maintaining the myth of war requires silence from those who know war's reality. Because people who find meaning in patriotism do not want to hear the truth of war, those who can tell us the truth are silenced… or they prefer to forget. Many veterans are discarded, shunted aside, and left to feel misunderstood and alone. "The shame and alienation of combat soldiers, coupled with the indifference to the truth of war by those who were not there, reduces many societies to silence."[8] And so:

> Each generation again responds to war as innocents. Each gen-

eration discovers its own disillusionment—often after a terrible price. The myth of war and the drug of war wait to be tasted.[9]

Larry Gwin went to combat in Vietnam as an innocent. In telling the story of his "baptism," he breaks the silence and helps dismantle the myth of war. His is an action story, and (dare I say it?) a guy story, one that most women would not particularly want to read. What I especially appreciate is the subtlety of the narrative as Larry brings the reader along on his journey from initiation, to comprehension, to critique, to despair.

He writes with uncompromising candor as he chronicles his reactions and feelings. There is his anger when his company entered a village and began rounding up people:

Who the hell were we to march in and disrupt this hamlet— march in, tear it up looking for weapons, drag everyone out of their homes like Gestapo in the night, and send the men off somewhere to be interrogated? Maybe it was necessary. Maybe not. Who knew?... The wailing of those poor, terrified women seemed to stay with me all day.[10]

There is his helplessness:

The dazed civilians ignored me. The medics kept working, as hard as they could. One of the wounded was a young girl, maybe twelve. Her leg had been blown off above the knee. She was burned, too, and going into shock. "American doctor here!" I called again, wanting to shout it so loud that all the world would hear me, wanting my voice to calm and soothe those poor battered villagers, to explain away the folly, the pain, the madness of the stupid [expletive deleted] war.[11]

There is his ecstasy at pending liberation. Three hundred twenty-six pages into the book, after unspeakable horror and after being wounded, Larry describes "A Touch of Heaven."

And then it began to sink in. I didn't have to go out into the field anymore. I'd had my last operation. No more air assaults. No more hot LZs [Landing Zones]. No more getting shot at. No more traipsing through the jungle looking for bad guys. No more gut-wrenching fear. No more death and dying.

My God, I was going to make it! I was going to make it through my tour!... It was over.[12]

But it wasn't over. Short of officers, the captain directed Larry back into battle. He describes how he slowly became "unglued." As his company forged ahead and Larry remained behind to escort a prisoner to an uncertain and unprotected landing zone where a helicopter was touching down to pick up the enemy soldier, this is what happened:

The prisoner wasn't moving fast enough. He didn't want to go at all. He was fighting me, holding back as defiantly as he could. So I kicked him in the ass and started yelling at him. I was yelling at him and shoving him forward as we went. But he still wasn't moving fast enough So, I kicked him again, and he fell to his knees. "Get up, you [expletive deleted]!" I screamed at him. He shook his head no. I kicked him again, but he refused to get up. So, I literally dragged him off the ground, stood him up, shoved him forward and kicked him again. This time he started moving, and I pushed him and herded him as fast as I could to the waiting ship, its crew chief beckoning to us to move faster. Finally, I shoved that poor recalcitrant PAVN prisoner into the waiting arms of the crew chief, and together we managed to get the son of a bitch into the Huey.

As soon as he was in, I turned tail and sprinted back to the cover of the tree line, plopping down to the ground as soon as I got there, and turning to see the ship lifting off safely above the treetops. When I turned back and looked at the first sergeant, he was staring at me. He was shocked. He'd been shocked at what he'd just seen, and rightly so, and I realized with an acute sense of shame that I had definitely crossed the line. I'd lost it.

Then I got angry and stared back at him. I just stared. He'd learn. He'd learn soon enough. He'd learn how it felt to be scared. He'd learn to hate, too. I was sure of that. He'd find out what it was all about eventually, but the look on his face was something I've not forgotten all these years, and it told me a lot. I was close to the edge, but I didn't know it.[13]

Having been promised he was going home and now back in the midst of danger, Larry reached the end of his strength:

And there we waited. After the barrage, we were simply going to stand up and charge across the open field to our front, charge the bunkers and the trench line in the woods across the way, charge across a hundred meters of open ground. That's when I'd get it, I knew. Charging across the open ground. I was too tired to fight it. Too tired to care. Too bloody sick of the bloody [expletive deleted] war to worry about it. I just didn't care.[14]

The title of this chapter is "One Last Picnic." Larry is good at irony. (We met when, as best man in a wedding party, he handed me a tumbler full of the water I requested, saying, "Your gin, Reverend.") I have sometimes wondered if a sense of irony isn't what got him through Vietnam.

Shortly before leaving Da Nang, Larry Gwin was promoted—to Captain. He writes:

It made a difference, somehow, coming home a captain. My dad had been a captain once, and my grandfather, and my grandfather's father. It meant a lot.[15]

Here is the lure and the danger: the military promotion meant a lot to this soldier, it gave him meaning despite (and maybe because of) the hell he had experienced.

I know up close and personal about the evil of war, something I never otherwise would have known, because for a time I was part of Larry Gwin's struggle to recover from a waking nightmare. To this day I feel privileged and blessed for my time with him in the early/mid eighties.

The need of Larry and all veterans to readjust to civilian life calls to mind Homer's character Odysseus, who was to return from war to the domestic life he left twenty years earlier. Chris Hedges discusses the *Iliad* and the *Odyssey*, saying, "No two works have come closer to chronicling the rage and consumption of war and the struggle to recover." Hedges notes that "the name *Odysseus* is tied to the Greek verb *odussomai,* which means 'to suffer pain.'"[16] To me Larry's pain was holy. He had been baptized into evil, and long after its end, he was struggling with the demons of war. His new challenge was to recover, somehow, a sense of the sacred. I could share my faith in God's compassion and goodness, but I could not share his horrific memories. As psychologist James Hillman puts it, PTSD carriers "are like initiates among innocents."[17] To read *Baptism* when it was finally completed and published was to understand a little better.

When history is taught, time is marked and divided by our wars, a fact that supports Hedges's point that war provides a common struggle, an opportunity to be noble and heroic. Peace activist Ruth Jacobs imagines a different world and wonders—

> Suppose, rather than teaching history as a series of prewar, war and postwar eras, schools teach history as a series of peace eras disrupted by destructive wars. Suppose books celebrate peace presidents and other peacemakers instead of war presidents and generals, emphasizing war casualties instead of victories. Suppose our elders speak at schools about the horrors of wars witnessed in their lifetimes.[18]

By turning things upside down here and offering an alternative perspective, Jacobs helps us to see how gender-based our history (his-story) has been. In a patriarchal culture, perhaps part of our problem is that

> The word peace has been associated among other things with passivity, un-manliness, subservience, namby pambiness, impotent idealism, cowardice, preachiness, stagnation, and considered an impediment to both creativity and competitiveness. Perhaps instead of putting our attention to "peace," we should focus on

understanding the forces that drive the human animal and developing skills to recognize these forces in operation and then learn how to handle them and concentrate on "negotiation" or "arbitration" or "forcing change" or some other word that means aggressive, realistic prevention of war.[19]

Hope for changing things, for achieving human community and a more peaceful world, depends in part upon gaining a better understanding of human motivation and behavior. Fortunately, social scientists are learning more about the roots of violence. Studies like James Gilligan's *Violence: Our Deadly Epidemic and Its Causes*[20] offer insight that complements and supports religious faith. To me, new knowledge and its dissemination in the proliferation of peace academies and peace studies programs signal progress toward the kingdom on earth for which Jesus prayed and are a sign that "God is still speaking."

In a final chapter of his book, Chris Hedges expresses his conviction that love alone gives us meaning that endures. I am reminded of Larry and his present sense of well-being. He concluded a recent e-mail message to me saying, "All family members are well and happy, too. What more could one hope for?! (The Big Ranger has been very good to me.)"

---

[1] Larry Gwin, *Baptism: A Vietnam Memoir.* New York: Ivy Books, 1999, p. 13.

[2] R. W. Apple Jr., "McCain, Trying His Best Not to Look Back," *The New York Times,* August 31, 2004, p. P1.

[3] Chris Hedges, *War Is a Force That Give Us Meaning.* New York: Anchor Books, 2003, p. 10.

[4] Ibid., p. 3.

[5] Ibid.

[6] Ibid., p. 22.

[7] Ibid., p. 40.

[8] Ibid., p. 176.

[9] Ibid., p. 173.

[10] Gwin, pp. 271–272.

[11] Ibid., p. 278.

[12] Ibid., p. 326.

[13] Ibid., pp. 333–334.

[14] Ibid., p. 344.

[15] Ibid., pp. 349–350.

[16] Hedges, p. 12.

[17] James Hillman, *A Terrible Love of War.* New York: Penguin Books, 2004, p. 32.

[18] Ruth Jacobs, "Epilogue: From Warpower to Peacepower" in *We Speak for Peace: An Anthology,* Ruth Harriet Jacobs, ed. Manchester, Connecticut: Knowledge, Ideas & Trends, Inc., 1993, p. 321.

[19] Joan Valdina, "The Word Peace," in *We Speak for Peace,* p. 291.

[20] James Gilligan, Violence: *Our Deadly Epidemic and Its Causes.* New York: G. P. Putnam's Sons, 1996.

KEYS TO ACHIEVING A WORLD CULTURE OF PEACE

Peace always seems a weary way off. As Jeremiah lamented,
"We looked for peace, but no peace came."
But to give up on peace is to give up on God.

The Reverend William Sloane Coffin[1]

We have begun by considering obstacles to peace—the negative. The task now is to consider keys to achieving peace—the positive. One woman who focused on the positive was Emily Greene Balch (1867–1961), co-founder with Jane Addams of the oldest women's peace organization in the world—the Women's International League for Peace and Freedom (1915). Balch was awarded the Nobel Peace Prize in 1946, just after the United States stunned and terrified the world by dropping a wholly new kind of bomb on Hiroshima and Nagasaki. Balch's Nobel Prize acceptance speech gives evidence of her approach to justice and peace work:

A dark and terrible side of this sense of community of interests is the fear of a horrible common destiny which in these days of atomic weapons darkens men's minds all around the globe. Men have a sense of being subject to the same fate, of being all in the same boat. But fear is a poor motive to which to appeal, and I am sure that "peace people" are on a wrong path when they expatiate on the horrors of a new world war. Fear weakens the nerves and distorts the judgment. It is not by fear that mankind must exorcise the demon of destruction and cruelty, but by motives more reasonable, more humane, and more heroic.[2]

Balch's wise words are as applicable today as they were at the end of World War II. If our goal is to encourage others to become peace activists, fanning fear of terrorism and terrorists is a poor motivator. To motivate people in ways that are more reasonable, humane, and even heroic, we must help them identify and work toward "the things that make for peace."

In the four chapters in this section, I offer my best thinking on the subject after more than two decades in ministry. For their critical roles in shaping my thoughts, I credit the Reverend William Sloane Coffin, former Yale University chaplain whose witness and discipleship has been a guide to me, and Ithaca College Protestant Community students, whom I have endeavored to guide.

A critical step toward peacemaking—one that usually does not come naturally and so is a challenge to many people of faith—is to **embrace diversity** (Chapter 8).

Once one has accepted the Other as a valued and respected equal, one is compelled to **work for equality and justice** (Chapter 9). All three faith traditions teach that there can be no peace without justice. A just and equitable sharing of the world's resources is a prerequisite to peace.

To **practice forgiveness and reconciliation** (Chapter 10) is perhaps the most difficult step in peacemaking. Following in God's way of compassion, mercy, and forgiveness, made known by Jesus' life and teachings, is the only way to break cycles of revenge and retribution.

Listening and telling stories of our lives and faith is another key way toward building human unity and peace across the faith traditions. To **engage in interfaith dialogue and cooperation** (Chapter 11) is to connect with one another in building bridges of understanding that can lead to common action. Even painful encounters can serve a useful purpose if they lead to greater grasp of the issues, better cooperation, increased respect for the Other, or deeper knowledge of God and Self. In the words of Paul, "We know that all things work together for good for those who love God, who are called according to his purpose" (Romans 8:28, NRSV).

---

[1] William Sloane Coffin, *Credo.* Louisville: Westminster John Knox Press, 2004, p. 91.

[2] Irwin Abrams, ed., *The Words of Peace: Selections from the Speeches of the Winners of the Nobel Peace Prize.* New York: Newmarket Press, 1990, pp. 4-5.

8

EMBRACE DIVERSITY

Human beings have a tendency to seek their own kind, or "tribe." We are apt to be most comfortable with people who are like ourselves. Yet, if the aim is to create a world culture of peace, we must learn to live with difference. More than that, we must learn to *value* difference. Unfortunately, this is a critical first step that many people of faith are not quite prepared to take. We resist moving out of our "comfort zone." We tend to fear and avoid the unknown. Encountering the Other takes some courage.

What strategies are available to religious leaders for encouraging Christians, Muslims, and Jews to *want* to engage difference? Perhaps the most powerful incentive is lifting up pluralism—our human many-ness—as a precious gift of the Creator. If we are persuaded that it is our Maker's plan for our lives to be enriched, enhanced, broadened, and deepened by those who are not like us, we are more likely to risk encountering the Other. In trust and faith in the will of God/Allah, we can move out (like Abraham and Sarah, and Ruth and Naomi) into unknown territory.

One person who did that is M. Thomas Thangaraj, a professor of world Christianity at Candler School of Theology. He was born in the small Christian village of Nazareth in South India, which maintained an intentionally protected Christian identity and environment by living separately from Hindus and the Hindu faith. Later, Thangaraj moved to the multireligious, urban settings of Madras and Calcutta, where he met Muslim and Hindu friends. They "nudged" him to look for other ways of relating to them and their religions than the one he grew up with.

Thangaraj did so and in his important little book *Relating to*

People of Other Religions: What Every Christian Needs to Know, he makes a compelling case for plurality and multiplicity in the universe as a gift of God. In an opening chapter, "God Saw That It Was Good!" Thangaraj draws upon the biblical story of God and God's mighty acts to show that "the whole creative act of God is a celebration of the many." From Genesis to Revelation, Scripture clearly shows that God has a great love for variety and difference, the professor persuasively argues. "Here is a God who is not satisfied with a singular expression of faith and obedience, but rather invites people of all nations to come to the feast and celebrate variety and difference."[1]

Jonathan Sacks, the Chief Rabbi of England, won the prestigious Grawemeyer Religion Award for his book *The Dignity of Difference: How to Avoid the Clash of Civilizations.* He notes that a primordial instinct going back to humanity's tribal past makes us see difference as a threat, but in an age where our destinies are linked, that instinct is "massively dysfunctional." In our time many want to focus on universal human characteristics, our commonalities. In Sacks's view this movement toward universalism has important functions, but we must take care to attend to the particular:

> A global culture is a universal culture, and universal cultures, though they have brought about great good, have also done immense harm. They see as the basis of our humanity the fact that we are all ultimately the same. We are vulnerable. We are embodied creatures. We feel hunger, thirst, fear, pain. We reason, hope, dream, aspire. These things are all true and important. But we are also different. Each landscape, language, culture, community is unique. Our very dignity as persons is rooted in the fact that none of us—not even genetically identical twins— is exactly like any other.[2]

Sacks urges us, therefore, to open ourselves to persons who think, act, and interpret reality in ways radically different from our own.

Peacemakers everywhere face the challenge of finding resourceful ways of bringing together people of different races, religions, and ethnicities. As they endeavor to break down the walls that divide us, open minds, and build bridges of understanding, their task is to create situations where people learn to accept, respect, and even embrace one another.

At the young and impressionable age of sixteen, I was deeply influenced by the goals of an international organization committed to achieving world peace through intercultural exchange. Their motto is "Walk Together, Talk Together. Only then will there be Peace." My lifelong commitment to bridging the boundaries that divide people was shaped then. It is a story I want to share with you.

Following World War II, the American Field Service (AFS) launched a visionary program for teenagers, designed to nurture world citizens by developing international friendships.[3] In 1947, fifty students were brought to the United States to live with host families and to attend their senior year in high school. These teenagers learned firsthand about the customs, ideals, and problems of American life while telling host communities about their own countries, customs, and traditions. Three years later, in 1950, the Americans Abroad program began when the AFS sent nine American students to other countries. The AFS exchange program grew quickly and became a great success. By 1959, when I became an AFSer, 1,109 American high school students traveled abroad and 1,525 teenagers came to live and study in the United States.

I had the incredible opportunity in the summer between my junior and senior years in high school to be an AFS exchange student to Finland. In this exquisite land of ten thousand lakes, I first experienced sauna and the midnight sun. I stayed with two families—one Swedish-speaking, one Finnish-speaking—and was introduced to the history of the bilingual nation. I attended church with my Lutheran pastor father, whose name was Frei, and my mother Ruth, brother Stig-Olaf, and sister Birgitta. I learned how yogurt is made, ate fish soup, indulged in lots of pastry, and gained ten pounds. In Finland, I wore wooden clogs, discovered Marimekko dresses and stopped wearing make-up... permanently. Even though

I had had times of homesickness, by summer's end I was not ready to come home.

During this first venture out of my country, I had come to view it differently. This was the late fifties, a time when *The Ugly American*, a book by William J. Lederer and Eugene Burdick, was making waves.[4] I read about how people in other countries often view Americans, especially xenophobic Americans traveling abroad. I felt there was truth to the perception that Americans feel entitled to more than their fair share of the world's wealth and resources; that Americans abroad can be inconsiderate, thoughtless, and arrogant; and that a U.S. passport offers special status and protection. I had to come to terms with my own learned prejudices—the notion that Americans value individual life more than other peoples do, that the American government will go to extraordinary, even heroic, lengths to protect American lives because Americans somehow count more. As a young person, I had the eye-opening experience of viewing America and the American character in a new and more critical way.

The experience of seeing things differently continued upon my return home. While I was still in Finland, an American Field Service exchange student had come to live with my family in Connecticut during our senior year in high school, 1959–1960. Raja nor Mahani is from the royal family of Malaysia, and she is a Muslim. Mahani wore saris, retired to her bedroom to pray, and, while observing the lunar month of fasting, taught us about Ramadan.

So it was—thanks to AFS—that interfaith dialogue and an understanding of Islam began for me at a very early age. This was not textbook learning, but lived, human experience of otherness. Strangely enough, Mahani and I did not feel as close to one another at that time as we did forty years later, after we both had become mothers. She returned for our fortieth high school reunion in 2000 and brought her daughter Aswina, a lawyer who studied in England. Over a visit of several days Mahani and I talked excitedly about our feminist faith commitments and projects, she movingly described to me her life-changing *haj* (pilgrimage) to Mecca, and we made plans to work out an exchange between Muslim women in Malaysia and Christians in the United States, *Insha'Allah*, God willing.

But before Mahani and I would see one another again, my nephew Nathaniel from Massachusetts would visit her daughter Aswina in Malaysia. My younger sister and I still marvel at the fact that the friendship we had with Mahani in high school would blossom many years later into friendship between her son and Mahani's daughter. This is not, of course, a surprise to the AFS, for enduring international connection and friendship is what was hoped and planned for all along.

At the time of Nathaniel's visit to Malaysia, he was working for a company in Singapore, having just completed two years of service in the Peace Corps in Senegal. The Peace Corps was a product of the sixties, that time of transformation born of great dreams and hope. It was a program introduced in March 1961 by President John F. Kennedy to help foreign countries meet their needs for skilled people power. Like the American Field Service it was designed to have Americans living with the nationals of the country in which they are stationed—doing the same work, eating the same food, talking the same language. In announcing the pilot program President Kennedy remarked, "The responsibility for peace is the responsibility of our entire society." He explained that every Peace Corps worker "will know that he or she is sharing in the great common task of bringing to man that decent way of life which is the foundation of freedom and a condition of peace."[5]

The era of President Kennedy was the era of the Cold War when the conflict with the Soviet Union and nuclear arms race was the greatest threat to world peace. Just months before his assassination, at American University in June 1963, Kennedy urged all Americans to re-examine their own attitudes toward the possibility of peace:

Too many of us think it is impossible. Too many think it unreal. But that is a dangerous, defeatist belief. It leads to the conclusion that war is inevitable—that mankind is doomed—that we are gripped by forces we cannot control.

We need not accept that view. Our problems are man-made—therefore, they can be solved by man. And man can be as big as he wants. No problem of human destiny is beyond human beings. Man's reason and spirit have often solved the seemingly unsolvable—and we believe they can do it again.[6]

President Kennedy acknowledged that the U.S. and the Soviet Union had real differences, but he appealed to common interests:

If we cannot end now our differences, at least we can help make the world safe for diversity. For, in the final analysis, our most basic common link is that we all inhabit this small planet. We all breathe the same air. We all cherish our children's future. And we are all mortal.[7]

In closing his address the President quoted the Bible:

"When a man's ways please the Lord," the Scriptures tell us, "he maketh even his enemies to be at peace with him." And is not peace, in the last analysis, basically a matter of human rights—the right to live out our lives without fear of devastation—the right to breathe air as nature provided it—the right of future generations to a healthy existence?

While we proceed to safeguard our national interest, let us also safeguard human interests. And the elimination of war and arms is clearly in the interest of both.[8]

About forty years later, in May 2004, Christian theological schools in the Washington, D.C., area took a pioneering step in helping to make the world safe for diversity when they voted unanimously to link an Islamic seminary to their active educational and fellowship programs. With this vote, students preparing for the Muslim ministry will be sharing classes with men and women studying to be Christian priests and pastors. David Yount, vice chairman of the Washington Theological Consortium (comprised of Baptist, Catholic, Episcopal, Lutheran, United Methodist, and Presbyterian seminaries), explains that the decision was driven, in part, by the fact that the School of Islamic Social Studies in

Leesburg, Virginia, trains Muslim chaplains for the U.S. armed forces. Every chaplain, regardless of his or her faith, is responsible to minister to the spiritual needs of every American serviceman and woman. But, he notes, there were deeper motives for the Christian seminaries to affiliate with the Muslim school:

Rather than shrink from the tragedies of 9/11 as portending a religious "clash of civilizations" between West and East, the collaboration affirms that Christianity, Islam and Judaism share a common origin in the person of the patriarch Abraham, as well as common values that override the differences that separate the three great world faiths. . . . Now future priests and ministers will be studying Islam on its home ground and future imams will be introduced to Christianity in Christian seminaries. Over time, the effort might disarm any clash of civilizations.[9]

One of my favorite writers on matters of Christian faith is the award-winning author, Anne Lamott. In thinking about the need to embrace diversity, I am taken by her simple statement about what it means to be saved—"If we are to believe Jesus or Gandhi, specifically [to be saved] means to see everyone on earth as family."[10]

I share Lamott's faith "that we are connected, and that everyone—everyone—eventually falls into the hands of God."[11] Lamott tells of her dying friend Sue, who had the following experience:

Some of her evangelical friends had insisted sorrowfully that her nieces wouldn't get into heaven, since they were Jews, as was one of her sisters. I told her what I believe to be true—that there was not one chance in a million that the nieces wouldn't go to heaven, and if I was wrong, who would even want to go?[12]

To me, evidence of pinched, ungodly, all-too-human, tribal, exclusivist thinking is that only people who believe as I do will be saved and go to heaven. When one sees everyone on earth as family, it is not difficult to believe that "everyone—everyone—eventually falls into the hands of God."

---

[1] Thomas Thangaraj, *Relating to People of Other Religions: What Every Christian Needs to Know.* Nashville: Abingdon Press, 1997, p. 28.

[2] Jonathan Sacks, *The Dignity of Difference: How to Avoid the Clash of Civilizations.* New York: Continuum, 2002, p. 47. *The Dignity of Difference* was first released in hardcover in 2002 and then reissued in a revised paperback edition, with a new preface, in 2003.

[3] As a volunteer ambulance service founded during World War I and active again in World War II, the AFS had the experience of carrying thousands of wounded soldiers of many nationalities and beliefs. The idea of a peacetime program to further friendship and understanding between peoples came to fruition with the establishment of American Field Service International Scholarships. For more information, go to *www.afs.org.*

[4] William J. Lederer and Eugene Burdick, *The Ugly American.* New York: W. W. Norton & Company, Inc., 1958. This was made into a film in 1963, *The Ugly American*, starring Marlon Brando, and was released as a DVD in 2003.

[5] "The Peace Corps" in *"Let the Word Go Forth," The Speeches, Statements, and Writings of John F. Kennedy, 1947-1963*, Theodore C. Sorensen, ed. New York: Delacorte Press, 1988, pp. 60-61.

[6] Ibid., "The Strategy of Peace," p. 283.

[7] Ibid., p. 286.

[8] Ibid., p. 289.

[9] "Muslim-Christian alliance created," *Finger Lakes Times*, June 11, 2004, p. 4A. Another Muslim school in Virginia has been in recent news stories—The Islamic Saudi Academy of Alexandria—where American citizen Ahmed Omar Abu Ali was valedictorian of his graduating class in 1999. Abu Ali was held without charge for twenty months in Saudi Arabia, transferred to the United States, and is accused of plotting to assassinate President Bush.

[10] Anne Lamott, *Plan B: Further Thoughts on Faith.* New York: Riverhead Books, 2005, p. 260.

[11] Ibid., p. 262.

[12] Ibid., p. 269.

9

WORK FOR EQUALITY AND JUSTICE

Citizens of the United States were shocked, repulsed, and ashamed when the mistreatment of detainees at Abu Ghraib prison in Iraq was revealed in the spring of 2004. Acts of humiliation and torture on the part of U.S. military seemed incomprehensible to citizens of a country whose Declaration of Independence states: "We hold these truths to be self evident, that all men are created equal." The guiding principle of "liberty and justice for all"—the human dignity and rights of every individual—is what, ostensibly, the U.S. wanted to export to Iraq and the entire world.

The tactic used by military intelligence to break down people so that they would offer information in the "fight" against terrorism was humiliation. A person's deep human need for dignity and respect was attacked. Prisoners were made to act like animals, crawling on hands and knees. They were stripped naked. Men were made to wear women's underwear on their heads. Women were made to bare their breasts. People were told to eat food out of a toilet and excrement was put on their bodies. The abuse was not only physical and psychological but also spiritual: men were forced to drink alcohol and eat pork, a desecration in Muslim law. Photos were taken and videos were made to record the violation.

When the photos and videos became public, Americans were incredulous. How could this happen? How could U.S. soldiers do such despicable things? Lessons of behavioral science and twentieth-century history taught that one could more readily brutalize another human being when the Other is viewed as less than human. The Ku Klux Klan called Americans of African descent "coons" and lynched them. Nazis called Jews "vermin" and gassed them. Some American soldiers called Iraqis "hajis" and tortured them. (In Islam the title *haji* is one of honor, given to Muslims who have made the pilgrimage to Mecca, the *haj*. The *haj* is required of all Muslims at least once in their lifetime and is the fifth pillar of Islam.)

No nation, people, or religion is immune from such inhumanity, for it is part of the human condition. The Reverend Dr. James A. Forbes, Jr., pastor of The Riverside Church in New York City, embraces people of other faiths and cautions against nationalistic narrowness and religious self-righteousness. When asked in an interview with Bill Moyers about the violence and terrorism of a radical faction of Islam, Forbes remembered what Christians in the Ku Klux Klan did and observed, "As long as we can acknowledge that violence and terror are equal opportunity visitors, and that they visit all our traditions, at least we are not naïve in regards to the only bad people are bad people of others' traditions."[1]

A twenty-eight-year-old member of the Florida National Guard who served six months in Iraq, went home to Miami on a furlough, and then refused to return to his unit when the furlough ended. He was charged with desertion and court-martialed. He spoke with a journalist of his harrowing experience in Iraq:

"You just sort of try to block out the fact that they're human beings and see them as enemies. You call them hajis, you know? You do all the things that make it easier to deal with killing them and mistreating them." Later, upon reflection, "you come face to face with your emotions and your feelings and you try to tell yourself that you did it for a good reason. And if you don't find it, if you don't believe you did it for a good reason, then, you know, it becomes pretty tough to accept it—to willingly be a part of the war."[2]

If demonizing or objectifying the Other as subhuman is key to giving oneself permission to do violence and make war, then honoring and respecting the Other as an equal is key to rejecting war and making peace. Every religion recognizes some form of the "Golden Rule." To "*do unto others as you would have them do unto*

84

you" is to care for the Other as one equal to oneself.

Norman Rockwell painted his own rendering of the Golden Rule in a *Saturday Evening Post* cover for April 1, 1961. Depicted here—looking solemn, reverent, pensive, expectant, and hopeful—are all manner of common people. They are youth, adults, children in arms, and elderly. They are of various skin colors, dark and fair; various ethnicities as represented by dress and headgear; and various religions as represented by symbols including a cross, prayer beads, Torah scrolls, and a *kippa* (or *yarmulke*) worn by an old, bearded man. No one person seems any more important or valued than another. Two children are holding empty bowls. "Do Unto Others As You Would Have Them Do Unto You" is Rockwell's title. This is a compelling, visual image of human difference, dignity, and longing.

"If you want peace, you must work for justice" is a truism. Peace and justice are inextricably linked. When there are gross economic and social inequalities, when all do not have equal opportunity for life, liberty, and the pursuit of happiness, there will be unrest and upheaval.

Racial injustice has been an ugly fact of life in the United States—with slavery, then segregation, and racism. Progress was made with the Supreme Court's historic decision on May 17, 1954, in the case of Brown v. the Board of Education. When the court's earlier ruling that segregated schools were "separate but equal" was struck down (separate is inherently unequal and therefore unlawful), the way was opened for racial integration and justice.

On May 17, 2004, the fiftieth anniversary of the decision was observed with much fanfare. Reflecting on Brown v. the Board of Education, associate Supreme Court justice Stephen G. Breyer urged people to recollect the conditions of fifty years ago and to appreciate those whose struggles made the decision possible. He explained that before the decision the court read the Fourteenth Amendment's words "equal protection of the laws" as if they protected only the members of the majority race. With the 1954 decision, they read those words as those who wrote the amendment after the Civil War meant them—as offering the same protection to citizens of every race. Brown "helped us to understand that our Constitution was meant to create a democracy that worked not just on paper but in practice." Justice Breyer said that the message the court sent forth in 1954 is

> the belief that many millions of Americans of different races, religions and points of view can come together to create one nation.... The message sets a goal: we have made progress; we aspire to more.[3]

As it happened, the fiftieth anniversary of Brown v. the Board of Education was also the date when marriage for same-sex couples became legal in the Commonwealth of Massachusetts. Human rights activists noted this coincidence and declared it fortuitous. In their view, marriage for gay people represents another step forward in the movement for equality and social justice.

So it was that about seven weeks later two prominent women in Massachusetts chose July 4, Independence Day, to be married. Professor Diana Eck (fifty-eight), a professor of comparative religion and director of the Pluralism Project at Harvard, and her partner, the Reverend Dorothy Austin (sixty), an Episcopal priest, wed in Memorial Chapel at Harvard. The ceremony closed with singing "my country 'tis of thee, sweet land of liberty." Then the participants processed to the yard of Lowell House, the student residence where the two have served as co-masters for almost a decade. Some four hundred guests were invited to the celebration.

"These two women are deeply—and also widely—religious. And neither is willing to cede faith to the religious right," wrote syndicated columnist Ellen Goodman. She quoted both on same-sex marriage, something they never thought they would see in their lifetime. For Diana Eck it presents "the whole issue of how we cope with difference":

> My work is thinking about religious difference and whether we'll be able to work and live creatively with it. Religion is not some-

thing that should be divisive, to create ever more fractures in a society. Religions can work at bridge-building and connections.

For Dorothy Austin, "This is a moment of prophecy—of mercy, justice, love, comfort. We need religious traditions and the people in them." Austin remembered her late grandmother, who had blessed their union decades ago, saying, "Them that mind don't matter and them that matter won't mind." To which Ellen Goodman offers an "Amen."[4]

For women in the United States, the quest for equality and social justice has a very long history that continues to this day. Elizabeth Cady Stanton was an early leader who worked tirelessly for women's equality. In 1848, she helped to organize the first Women's Rights Convention held in Seneca Falls, New York, where she was living as a young wife and mother. Although Mrs. Stanton did not see women's suffrage in her lifetime (she died in 1902 and women did not receive the right to vote until 1920), she was never discouraged. Her persistence, patience, and ability to take the long view were exemplary. "I never forget that we are sowing winter wheat, which the coming spring will see sprout, and other hands than ours will reap and enjoy," she wrote.[5]

When she was seventy-eight years old, Elizabeth Cady Stanton was asked to address the Parliament of World Religions gathering in Chicago. Equality for all people was very much on her mind when she wrote her paper, delivered in October 1893. Mrs. Stanton said:

The prophets and apostles alike taught a religion of deeds rather than forms and ceremonies. "Away with your new moons, your sabbaths and your appointed feasts; the worship God asks is that you do justice and love mercy." "God is no respecter of persons." "He has made of one blood all the nations of the earth." When the pulpits in our land shall preach from these texts and enforce these lessons, the religious con-science of the people will take new form of expression, and those who in very truth accept the teachings of Jesus will make it their first duty to look after the lowest stratum of humanity....

For peace and prosperity in their conditions we must begin with the lowest stratum of society and see that the masses are well fed, clothed, sheltered, educated, elevated and enfranchised....

Those who train the religious conscience of the people must teach the lesson that all these artificial distinctions in society must be obliterated by securing equal conditions and opportunities for all: this cannot be done in a day; but this is the goal for which we must strive. The first step to this end is to educate the people into the idea that such a moral revolution is possible....

"Equal rights for all" is the lesson this hour.

Mrs. Stanton knew that there would be some who would object, and say, "If you should distribute all things equally to-day they would be in the hands of the few to-morrow." To this she would reply, "Not if the religious conscience of the people were educated to believe that the way to salvation was not in creed and greed, but in doing justice to their fellow men."[6]

Jane Addams, another leader in the first wave of the women's movement, was a justice and peace activist. Writing in 1907, after an International Peace Conference was held in Boston in 1904, she observed a new internationalism. Not knowing what to call this sentiment, she felt "driven to the rather absurd phrase of '*cosmic patriotism.*'"

> Whatever it may be called, it may yet be strong
> enough to move masses of men out of their narrow
> national considerations and cautions into new reaches
> of human effort and affection.[7]

Like Mrs. Stanton, Addams grounded her thought upon the Bible. She spoke of the witness of the Hebrew prophet Isaiah:

He contended that peace could be secured only as men abstained from the gains of oppression and responded to the cause of the poor; that swords would finally be beaten into plowshares and pruning hooks, not because men resolved to be peaceful, but because all the metal of the earth would be turned to its proper use when the poor and their children should be abundantly fed. It was as if the ancient prophet foresaw that under an enlightened industrialism peace would no longer be an absence of war, but the unfolding of worldwide processes making for the nurture of human life.[8]

More than a century later "Equal rights for all" is still the lesson of the hour. As justice seekers and peacemakers, we can draw encouragement from the words and actions of sisters gone before. We can also draw inspiration from one another. I think of Sahir Dajani, a Muslim woman of Jerusalem. "Her credo for peace includes the solid conviction that no one person is better than any other."[9]

---

[1] From *Speaking to Power, NOW with Bill Moyers Special Edition.* Broadcast December 26, 2003, on PBS. © Public Affairs Television. All rights reserved.

[2] An Op-Ed piece by Bob Herbert, "Gooks to Hajis," in *The New York Times,* May 21, 2004, p. A23.

[3] Stephen G. Breyer, "50 Years After Brown, A Decision That Changed America Also Changed the Court," Op-Ed article, *The New York Times,* May 17, 2004, p. A25.

[4] Ellen Goodman, "This gay marriage challenges religious divide," *Finger Lakes Times,* Sunday, July 4, 2004, p. D1.

[5] Elisabeth Griffith, *In Her Own Right: The Life of Elizabeth Cady Stanton.* Oxford University Press, 1984, p. 208.

[6] John Henry Barrows, *The World's Parliament of Religions,* volume 2, Chicago: Parliament Publishing Co., 1893, pp. 1235–1236.

[7] From "Newer Ideals for Peace," in *The Power of Nonviolence: Writings by Advocates of Peace.* Boston: Beacon Press, 2002, p. 40.

[8] Ibid., p. 41.

[9] Ann N. Madsen, writing about Sahir Dajani in *Making Their Own Peace: Twelve Women of Jerusalem,* New York: Lantern Books, 2003, p. 173.

10

PRACTICE FORGIVENESS AND RECONCILIATION

With the advent of rocket science and the space age, humanity has been given the gift of a wholly new perspective on our globe. The first astronauts to view the earth from outer space reported its beauty as nearly indescribable and told of their sense of awe and reverence. A photographic image of the earth taken from space is now reproduced on a blue flag, which is a symbol, like the United Nations flag, of one world. Inspired by this image, Jane Parker Huber has written a wonderful "Hymn for Peacemaking 1992." It is sung to the tune Hyfrydol (the tune of "Praise the Lord, Ye Heavens Adore Him"):

When, in awe of God's creation, We view earth from outer space
This mysterious, floating marble, Strewn with clouds and bathed in grace!
How can we not pause in wonder Seeing earth as one and whole,
Then, confessing our divisions, Make earth's healing our prime goal.
Blue and tan, with lace clouds swirling, Flung in space and circling there,
Habitat for myriad creatures Meant for earth and sea and air!

Must we draw our lines of hatred Marking land and class and race?
God, forgive us, we entreat You, For all pride of self and place.

Living now, this is the picture, We no longer can deny,
For we see no angry boundaries When our view is from the sky
Rivers, deserts, forests, snowfields, Oceans, lakes and mountains, too
But no fences built for barring You from me or me from you.

Now we face the unknown future, Challenged by the work at hand.
Still the God of all creation Summons us with One Command:
"Love each other!" Will we do it? "Love each other!" Wars might cease!
"Love each other!" Justice follows; "Love each other!" There is peace![1]

©Jane Parker Huber. All rights reserved. Used by permission.

To "make earth's healing our prime goal" will mean breaking ancient cycles of revenge, retaliation, and retribution. It will mean rising to the tough spiritual challenge of practicing forgiveness and reconciliation. "How quickly we take offense, we escalate offense, we magnify offense, we return offense," Professor Diana Eck, director of the Pluralism Project at Harvard, observes of human behavior.[2] That's so true, sadly.

For Christians, God's call to forgiveness is at the heart of the faith. Jesus taught us to say when we pray, "And forgive us our sins, for we ourselves forgive everyone indebted to us" (Luke 11:4, NRSV). And as he was dying on the cross Jesus prayed, "Father, forgive them; for they do not know what they are doing" (Luke 23:34, NRSV).

The words, "Father, forgive them," resonate at a deep level with Christians. They are often repeated, if not always followed. Followers of Christ believe that "they will know that we are Christians by our love." When a church member is acting toward another in a way that is particularly unloving or unforgiving, he or she is frequently criticized for being "unchristian" and exhorted to forgive as Jesus forgave.

In Paul's Letter to Philemon, a New Testament book a brief twenty-five verses long, we have a record of the apostle Paul making an appeal to a believer to act in the Lord Jesus' way of love and reconciliation. Paul is sending the slave Onesimus back to his master Philemon; and the letter, intended to accompany him, makes a plea on Onesimus's behalf. Although the precise nature of Paul's request is uncertain, what is clear is that Paul is making an all-out effort to be persuasive, to convince Philemon to do as he asks.

Paul begins by addressing Philemon as co-worker and brother:
When I remember you in my prayers, I always thank my God because I hear of your love for all the saints and your faith toward the Lord Jesus. I pray that the sharing of your faith may become effective when you perceive all the good that we may do for Christ. (verses 4-6, NRSV)

Although Paul is bold enough in Christ to "command" Philemon to do his "duty," Paul would rather appeal to him "on the basis of love" (verses 8-9, NRSV). He writes Philemon regarding Onesimus:

I am sending him, that is, my own heart, back to you. I wanted to keep him with me, so that he might be of service to me in your place during my imprisonment for the gospel; but I preferred to do nothing without your consent, in order that your good deed might be voluntary and not something forced. Perhaps this is the reason he was separated from you for a while, so that you might have him back forever, no longer as a slave but more than a slave, a beloved brother—especially to me but how much more to you, both in the flesh and in the Lord.

So if you consider me your partner, welcome him as you would welcome me. If he has wronged you in any way, or owes you anything, charge that to my account.

(verses 12-18, NRSV)

Paul's appeal to Philemon for reconciliation with Onesimus (and according to one interpretation, for forgiveness of his transgressions) is a public one. Fellow Christians and missionaries whom Paul names will observe Philemon's decision; they are onlookers. Paul engages in strenuous arm-twisting here, then closes, "The grace of the Lord Jesus Christ be with your spirit" (verse 25, NRSV).

Many Christians believe and will argue that Jesus' exhortation to forgiveness and reconciliation distinguishes Christianity from other religions. Sahir Dajani, a devout Muslim woman living in Jerusalem, would not disagree. She speaks about distinctive value in her own religion, forgiveness in Christianity, and the good to be found in all religions:

You believe in the values of your religion. So you try to adapt it to your philosophy and whatever good you do. I begin with the good values of Islam. There are values in each religion. So you have to look at the good values and then live accordingly.

93

But you also look at what is good in other religions. In Christianity, they forgive. Forgiveness is good! You realize that your religion does not have everything. You believe in forgiving, though you are not Christian. You must follow it because you try to do what's good and please God. You can seek good things from every place.[3]

One human being who is revered the world over for his capacity for forgiveness is Nelson Mandela. Incarcerated by South Africa's apartheid regime for twenty-seven long years (or ten thousand days), he astonished people on his release with his lack of bitterness. Those who had imprisoned him and whose power and abuses he had so long and courageously resisted could hardly believe it. They expected something quite different. Nelson Mandela was not an angry man. Although he carried scars of captivity in body and mind, he carried no hatred in his heart. He did not dwell on those lost years; rather, his thought was for the future.

I had the privilege of hearing Mr. Mandela speak at the Good Hope Arena when I visited Cape Town for the Parliament of World Religions meeting in 1999. I vividly remember that an usher stopped someone near me that night who wanted to take a flash photo. When the photographer objected, the usher patiently explained that Mr. Mandela had sustained eye injuries during his captivity on Robben Island and the flash would hurt him. The sense of protectiveness, reverence, and pride the South African felt toward his leader was evident.

Taking a high-speed tourist ferry to offshore Robben Island, site of the infamous prison now a museum, was the most extraordinary experience I had in South Africa. To see the tiny cell where Nelson Mandela was held prisoner and to go to the limestone quarry where he was forced to labor for thirteen years was a kind of pilgrimage. I learned that what permanently affected his eyesight was the blinding sunlight that shone off of the bright white quarry rock. Eager for more details of his story, and aware of a long airplane ride home, I bought a lightweight, abridged version of Mandela's autobiography, *Long Walk to Freedom*, at the ticket office/tourist shop on the Victoria and Albert waterfront.[4]

Nelson Mandela was seventy-one years old when he was released from prison on February 11, 1990. At dusk on the day of his release, he spoke to a huge crowd from a top-floor balcony of City Hall on the Grand Parade in Cape Town. Addressing the sea of exuberant people, he said:

> Friends, comrades and fellow South Africans, I greet you all in the name of peace, democracy and freedom for all! I stand here before you not as a prophet but as a humble servant of you, the people. Your tireless and heroic sacrifices have made it possible for me to be here today. I therefore place the remaining years of my life in your hands.[5]

Then he was driven to the home of Archbishop Desmond Tutu to spend his first night of freedom. Thousands of people lined the streets to greet him as the car passed.

The next day he flew by helicopter to a stadium in Soweto. There he addressed an overflow crowd of 120,000 cheering people. In closing, he opened his arms "to all South Africans of goodwill" and proclaimed, "No man or woman who has abandoned apartheid will be excluded from our movement towards a non-racial, united and democratic South Africa."[6]

Nelson Mandela worked with F. W. de Klerk for the new South Africa. De Klerk had been elected president in 1989. After just five months in office, on February 2, 1990, he announced on world-wide television his dramatic decision to release Mr. Mandela from prison and to legalize the previously banned African National Congress (ANC) and Communist Party. Together then, Mandela and de Klerk worked for the country's first democratic election. In June 1993, a date was set for the next year. It was the brink of a new era, and the 1993 Nobel Prize was awarded to Mandela and de Klerk jointly.

There was violence in the period before the election because there were people who did not want it to take place. But as Mr.

Mandela writes, "Mr. de Klerk and I stood firm" and Election Day came:

> It was a bright and clear day on 27 April 1994. On that day millions of South Africans, from every corner of the country, made their way to the polling stations to cast their vote in the country's first ever democratic election.
>
> The people stood patiently in long lines for their chance to vote for the party of their choice. There was a feeling of great joy in the air.
>
> Old men and women who had never voted before said that they felt like human beings for the first time in their lives. Everybody, both black and white, spoke of their pride to be living in a free country at last.[7]

That day Mr. Mandela, too, cast the first vote of his life. His party, the ANC, won a majority of the national vote; and in May he was sworn in as South Africa's first democratically elected president (Mr. de Klerk was sworn in as second deputy president). In *Long Walk to Freedom*, Mr. Mandela recalls the speech he made on that historic occasion in Pretoria, so long the seat of white power and control:

> I said that I believed that from the disaster of the past, a new society would be born which the world would be proud of. I spoke of how our victory belonged to everyone, for it was a victory for justice, for peace and for human dignity....
>
> I ended with the following words:
>
> "Never, never and never again shall it be that this beautiful land will again experience the oppression of one by another... the sun shall never set on so glorious a human achievement."[8]

To the outside world, South Africa's transformation is something of a miracle. Through the statesmanship of Mr. Mandela and Mr. de Klerk, the dismantling of apartheid happened through a political process. A revolution accomplished relatively peacefully, it has demonstrated what is possible and has given hope.

In his autobiography Nelson Mandela identifies himself as a freedom fighter. For him the freedom struggle is his life. Noticeably absent are references to God or to prayer, even in times of extremity—as after his trial when he is condemned to life in prison.

Mr. Mandela explains at the beginning of his book that both his parents were religious, but in different ways:

My father believed in Qamata, the God of his fathers and the great spirit of the Xhosa people. My mother, on the other hand, became a Christian and baptized me into the Methodist Church.[9]

He tells readers that his divorce from his first wife, Evelyn Mase, came about because their interests began to differ sharply. She became more religious, a Jehovah's Witness, while he became more "devoted to the ANC and the struggle."[10] Indeed, he is prepared to sacrifice to the death in freedom's cause. "No sacrifice was too great in the struggle for freedom,"[11] he writes. Nelson Mandela does not identify himself as a Christian. I was surprised and amazed when I realized this because his forgiveness of his enemies is so Christ-like, his behavior so exemplary.

I cannot help but think about Christians who believe that *only* Christians will be saved. The Gospel verse used as proof text is, of course, John 3:16:

For God so loved the world that he gave his only Son, so that everyone who believes in him may not perish but may have eternal life. (NRSV)

In Sunday school or vacation Bible school, children learn to say this verse by heart as a summary of Christian faith. For proselytizing Christians eager to convert people of other faiths, it is a touchstone. At sporting events, demonstrations, and rallies, you occasionally see placards proclaiming simply "John 3:16." Similarly, the reminder "John 3:16" is displayed on billboards, road signs, bumper stickers, and tee shirts.

Another proof text used is also from the Gospel of John: "I am the way, and the truth, and the life. No one comes to the Father except through me" (14:6, NRSV).

Is eternal life only for Christian believers? Will those who are not Christians perish? Is that the meaning of John 3:16? And 14:6?

No, absolutely not—at least not in my understanding. Will Nelson Mandela and all human beings like him who struggle for justice, human liberation, and peace in our world, but do not name Jesus as Lord, be excluded from God's kingdom? Will they be "left behind" at the second coming of Christ anticipated by so many believers? No, not in my understanding. Jesus lived and taught God's extravagant, universal love.

Well then, what do I make of John 3:16? I focus first on the "for God so loved the world" part. In our time we experience the unthinkable in horrific acts of terrorism and ethnic cleansing, acts that intentionally target innocent children, women, and men. We experience acts that confound our notions of love and nurture. A female terrorist deliberately shoots and kills a male parent as he runs forward to rescue a little child during the occupation of a school in Beslan, Russia (an occupation that was itself unthinkable). Women suicide bombers strap explosives to their bodies and blow themselves up, taking others with them—the more the better.

God so loved the world—What? What's next?—that God sent Jesus to reveal God's will for all human life. Ultimately, the only hope for breaking cycles of violence, whether personal or state-sponsored, is forgiving the unforgivable. It is by following the teachings of Jesus and by following his example that the world may be saved. And nothing less than the survival of the world is at stake in an age of nuclear arms and other weapons of mass destruction. Only IF we believe and act upon what Jesus taught us and what he demonstrated on the cross—that the way to peace is through love of enemies, forgiveness, and reconciliation—will we not perish.

In sum, this is what John 3:16 tells me: Jesus [*whom Christians call the*] Christ reveals the way. Practicing forgiveness and reconciliation is absolutely necessary if the world God so loves is to be saved. That, too, is the meaning of John 14:6. In response to Thomas's question, "Lord, we do not know where you are going. How can we know the way?" (14:5, NRSV), Jesus answers, "I am the way." The *way*—the way we are to live:

> This is my commandment, that you love one another as I have loved you. No one has greater love than this, to lay down one's life for one's friends. You are my friends if you do what I command you. (John 15:12-14, NRSV)

God's *way* of love is revealed by Jesus. "God is love, and those who abide in love abide in God, and God abides in them" (1 John 4:16, NRSV).

Perhaps I've got it wrong, but I don't think so. I believe that Christians who want to limit God's salvation to born-again Christians like themselves are not truly sharing the good news, the gospel. In God's extravagant love, each one of us is received, doctrinal flaws and all.

When leaders intent on peace and reconciliation reach out to one another, God's grace is experienced and even ancient and recurring conflicts between nations and/or peoples can be resolved. I am moved by a story told by Dr. Thomas E. Ambrogi, a human rights advocate and interfaith theologian, with an earlier history as a Jesuit priest and a university professor of theology and the applied social sciences.

Tom Ambrogi traveled to France with his wife for the sixtieth anniversary of the D-Day landings in June 2004. They laid flowers on a soldier's grave in the American cemetery on the high bluff above Omaha Beach, where nearly ten thousand Americans are buried. Later, at the Peace Memorial in Caen, they witnessed an exchange between French president Jacques Chirac and German Chancellor Gerhard Schroeder that was for Ambrogi the highlight of their trip. Returning home, he wrote "A New Europe at Normandy," an account of the exemplary statesmanship of these leaders and the promise it represents for finding a way where there seems no way, hope where things seem hopeless.[12]

In his essay Ambrogi explains that the presence of Chancellor Schroeder was a first. In sixty years no German leader had been invited to participate in a D-Day memorial. Standing beside

Jacques Chirac, Gerhard Schroeder (born in 1944) spoke for a new generation of Germans, people who have no personal memories of Nazi Germany.

The chancellor said, "France's memories of June 6, 1944 are different from Germany's. But they all end in a common conviction: We want peace."[13] He said that no one would ever forget the twelve years of Hitler's rule, that his generation grew up in its shadow. He never had a chance to know his father, who fell in Romania; the family had found his grave only four years earlier. "Out of nationalistic madness, the European partnership was born. Let us this day use these memories to further work for peace." The death sixty years ago of those who were "robbed of a happier life" was not in vain, for "we live in peace and freedom."

President Chirac responded that Mr. Schroeder represented the German people and that it was a moment of very great emotion:

You take upon yourself the memory of Germany. You incarnate it in a new Springtime. You were born when hope was being reborn. You belong to this generation born in the ruins, which has affirmed itself in its will to construct a new country....

Our ceremony today gives witness before the world that there is no conflict, however profound and painful, which cannot leave room one day for dialogue and understanding. To those who confront one another in the endless night of hatred and resentment, our reconciliation offers a genuine hope. Better still, it offers a choice. That of boldness, or courage, and of patience. There is always a possible path toward peace. Together, the German and French peoples have chosen to bear this message.

Jacques Chirac closed by saying to Gerhard Schroeder, "On this day of remembrance and of hope, French women and French men receive you more than ever as a friend. They receive you as a brother." And then the Frenchman reached out and gave the German a great bear hug.

The American observer notes that it is hard to fully appreciate the historic significance of this moment, after two centuries of conflict—Napoleon and his legions, the Franco-Prussian War, World War I, and World War II. Finally it was over.

The extraordinary pledge of reconciliation between the German and French leaders went almost unnoticed in the international media. But today Thomas Ambrogi bears witness, recalling the statesmen's message about the path to peace. He observes that if policymakers in Washington were to have ears to hear, "we just might move from an imperial future of endless war after preventive war to a world that is peacefully interconnected and interdependent."

Sometimes ancient hatreds and conflicts between peoples and nations are prolonged or go unresolved out of a misguided attempt to honor those who have given their lives for the cause. It is thought that to disengage would mean that the sacrifice of the dead would be in vain, and so the fight goes on. It is here that I find the words of Mr. Chirac at the D-Day ceremonies particularly pertinent. He remarked, "It is by its engagement in the service of peace and solidarity that Europe will be faithful to the memory of all those who have fallen here in the name of liberty."

We best honor the memory of all who have paid the ultimate price and sacrificed themselves in combat for the sake of future generations, by desisting from war and seeking political solutions. As the bumper sticker proclaims: "Peace is patriotic."

---

[1] "A Hymn for Peacemaking 1992," © Copyright 1992 Jane Parker Huber. Used by permission.

[2] "Difference Is No Excuse for Hatred," *Voices of the Religious Left: A Contemporary Sourcebook*, Rebecca T. Alpert, ed. Philadelphia: Temple University Press, 2000, p. 263.

[3] Ann N. Madsen, *Making Their Own Peace: Twelve Women of Jerusalem.* New York: Lantern Books, 2003, p. 170.

[4] Nelson Mandela, *Long Walk to Freedom: The Autobiography of Nelson Mandela*, abridged by Coco Cachalia and Marc Suttner. London, UK: Little, Brown and Co., Ltd., 1994.

[5] Ibid., p. 134.

[6] Ibid., p. 136.

[7] Ibid., p. 148.

[8] Ibid., p. 151.

[9] Ibid., p. 3.

[10] Ibid., p. 42.

[11] Ibid., p. 77.

[12] Published in *Fellowship, the journal of the Fellowship of Reconciliation*, November–December 2004. www.forusa.org/fellowship/nov-dec-04/ambrogi.html

[13] Ibid. Quotations in the rest of this chapter are from *Fellowship.*

11

ENGAGE IN INTERFAITH DIALOGUE
AND COOPERATION

The event that launched the worldwide interfaith movement was the World's Parliament of Religions held in 1893 in conjunction with the celebrated World's Fair in Chicago. Religious leaders of traditions other than Christianity—most all of them men—came from many countries and cultures, raising the awareness of Americans of that era to beliefs different from their own.

Not until one hundred years later, in 1993, was a second Parliament of World Religions held, also in Chicago. At the gathering of some seven thousand people, a Declaration of a Global Ethic, written mostly by men, was signed mostly by men. With few notable exceptions, the interfaith movement has been a movement led by males and, perhaps consequently, the primary focus in interreligious dialogue has been more on doctrine and creed, than relationship and experience.

The reader may have noticed that I have used the words *interfaith* and *interreligious* apparently interchangeably. Actually, the two words are not synonymous. Lawrence Whitney discovered the distinction while studying interreligious dialogue. (Because of his feminist desire to help promote women's equality and leadership, I make particular mention of this gifted young divinity student, who worked as an intern for the Women's Interfaith Institute during the summer between his junior and senior years in college.) Larry clarifies the distinction:

Interreligious describes a relationship between religious institutions or those representing religious institutions. Interfaith describes a relationship between individual persons at the level of belief.[1]

So it is that in naming our institute, for example, we used the word *interfaith* to indicate our intention to have women participate in dialogue and cooperation at the level of personal belief, rather than as representatives of particular religious traditions, although on occasion we do that as well.

Emerita Professor Mary Farrell Bednarowski, of the United Theological School of the Twin Cities in Minnesota, once told a remarkable story of an interfaith experience.[2] I include it here as an example of an approach to interfaith dialogue that tends to center upon personal, experiential sharing. Mary told her listeners:

Sometimes, sometimes, we have the great good fortune of an experience that gives us hope, gives us hope about these things that we're trying to learn, experience that changes our understandings of what might be possible.

I had an experience this summer that was profoundly like that. It was a Women's Interfaith Holocaust tour, in which twenty-one women—Jewish, Protestant, Catholic, black, and white women—traveled to Poland and the Czech Republic to be together in those places where such terrible things had happened that we were often speechless. In some mysterious way, we acquired a wisdom about how to be together, with our very different fears, and our very different kinds of courage, our very different life stories, and our religious traditions at stake.

Marsha Yugend, the Jewish woman who organized the tour, set the tone for that experience by saying, "We will enter Auschwitz as sisters." It gets to me all over again. "We will enter Auschwitz as sisters."

That statement of faith on her part helped us acquire the wisdom we needed, because we were afraid. We said to each other, by our presence on that tour:

We will be together in these places.

We will watch out for each other.

We will listen to whatever needs to be said.

We will not be fearful or anxious or prodding when it seems that silence is the only possible response.

We will wait for the slowest.

We will sooner or later catch up with the fastest.

We will dry the tears of those who are weeping and know they will dry ours when that time comes.

We will let ourselves begin to feel the pain—at least a little—of those we have considered our enemies, and we will let ourselves feel the pain of being thought of as someone else's enemy—not the pain of hurt feelings or of being misunderstood, but the pain of acknowledging all those strands of history that have put so many barriers between us.

We said to each other:

We will not forget the joy of life.

We will not forget to be grateful.

We will do our best to stir in each other the courage to act with love and justice in our own particular lives.

We said to each other:

We will be together in these places.

And we were.[3]

When women from diverse denominational and religious backgrounds come together to share their stories and to offer one another support in their faith journeys, as the women on this Holocaust tour surely did, they can be a powerful force for change. The seventies, eighties, and nineties witnessed a remarkable rise of women's spirituality groups across the nation. Women gathered in grassroots circles to share their faith and simple rituals. Some sought sisterhood as they challenged patriarchal practices within their churches.

During the early nineties I helped conduct a nationwide research study of the emerging phenomenon of women's spirituality groups. I worked with colleagues at the Hartford Seminary, Dr. Adair Lummis and Dr. Miriam Therese Winter, conducting interviews and designing, distributing, and digesting thousands of questionnaires. The results were published in *Defecting in Place: Women Claiming*

Responsibility for Their Own Spiritual Lives.[4] What was most striking to me was the ease with which women are crossing boundaries that have traditionally divided people. By sharing their struggles, hopes, and dreams, they discover what unites them, find their own voices, and become extremely creative in coming up with new forms of liturgy and expression.

My own participation in women's spirituality groups served as inspiration for the Women's Interfaith Institute (*www.womensinterfaithinstitute.org*). Working initially with Elaine Blondin Mello, and then with clergywomen in the Berkshire Hills of western Massachusetts, I founded a nonprofit organization in 1992 that has grown and flourished.

We are an organization of "women supporting women of diverse faiths in generating spiritual leadership, scholarship, and service." Members are clergy and lay, young and old, and represent different faiths, cultures, and ethnicities. Our programs include educational seminars, workshops, book groups, retreats, etc. Today we are two sister groups—in the Berkshires and in the Finger Lakes—that work closely together and hope to establish affiliate Women's Interfaith Institute centers in other locations.

Our home is in Seneca Falls, New York, a strategic place. The opportunity in 2002 to purchase a historic church located next door to the Women's Rights National Historical Park and down the street from the National Women's Hall of Fame seemed providential. Thousands of visitors come to Seneca Falls annually. As New York state senator Michael Nozollio wrote to us, "There is no better venue for an interfaith educational resource for women than the birthplace of women's rights."[5]

"Bringing Peace to Life" was the theme of the Institute's celebratory, opening weekend in June 2004. We sang a song of peace composed for the occasion by board member Madeline Hansen; and we dedicated a peace pole on our side lawn, where we could anticipate it would be noticed for years to come. Professor Maura O'Neill, author of *Women Speaking, Women Listening: Women in*

Interreligious Dialogue,[6] traveled from California to serve as our keynote speaker. Maura addressed three questions: Why interfaith? Why women? and Why now? Everyone privileged to be in the audience agreed that she was brilliant and that we could not have had a more auspicious beginning. We were dismayed to discover that her book, published in 1990, is out of print. I am happy to say that, partly influenced by her experience at our Institute in Seneca Falls, Maura has begun research on a new book, which, like *Women Speaking, Women Listening* promises to break ground and be an important contribution. Her working title is "Soulsister or Stepsister: Conflicting Feminisms and Their Effect on Interreligious Dialogue." The study is based on Maura's observations that women engaged in interreligious dialogue are, most often, from the more liberal or progressive sectors of their respective traditions, and that in many cases, these women have more in common with each other than they do with their sisters of the more traditional or conservative branches of their own traditions.

She explains, "This book explores the possibility and ramifications of dialoguing with the growing group of feminists from all traditions who espouse a more traditional approach to women's roles and identities. It is the premise of the book that such a dialogue is necessary in a world where conservative religion and politics are growing and the rift between both ideologies is getting wider and wider.... By making women's dialogue more inclusive there will be a greater possibility of real and lasting mutual understanding." (E-mail message to me from Maura O'Neill on July 25, 2005.)

I absolutely agree that the rift between ideologies is getting wider and wider. In my experience, gaining the interest of young college students in interfaith dialogue and cooperation is not at all easy. There are, of course, outstanding exceptions; but generally I have found committed Christian students to be quite conservative and unwilling to engage the Other. The only reason to be in dialogue, it seems, is to try to convert the Other. I have been deeply dismayed by this and have asked myself, Why? What's going on? I

107

think there is resistance because interfaith dialogue feels threatening. Young people seem afraid. What they don't know, what they have not experienced and I try to explain, is that interfaith dialogue usually works to deepen one's faith, not diminish or destroy it. In conversation with a person whose convictions are quite different, one is often forced to examine and learn more about one's own convictions and religious tradition. This can be, and usually is, a positive experience.

To be sure, to engage in interfaith dialogue, one must have an open mind. One must be prepared to be influenced by the Other. One must be willing to be changed. Often the change is to live one's tradition more faithfully and with more consciousness of its meaning.

In my many years in ministry, I have been delighted by the numbers of elders I have met whose minds are open, curious, and inquiring. And the numbers of young people I have worked with whose minds are closed has saddened me. This reversal of what I expected has been a huge surprise.

At those times when I become discouraged—when I begin to think that generating support for interfaith dialogue and cooperation is just too hard, that there is too little understanding and too much resistance—I recall the resistance that Jesus himself faced. We see an example of it in Luke's story about the opening of Jesus' ministry.

Just back in Galilee from his days apart in the desert where he had faced and mastered temptation, Jesus returned to his hometown of Nazareth. In the synagogue on the Sabbath day, he read from Isaiah, chapter 21: "The Spirit of the Lord is upon me, because he has anointed me to bring good news to the poor..." (Luke 4:18, NRSV). After reading the word, Jesus closed the book, and sat down for the question-and-answer time following the lesson. All eyes were upon him.

He then said to the people, "Today this scripture has been fulfilled in your hearing" (Luke 4:21, NRSV). Jesus' statement was shocking. He announced himself, in his hometown, as a prophet, one come to fulfill Scripture. How do they respond? At first, favorably. "All spoke well of him, and were amazed at the gracious words that came from his mouth" (4:22, NRSV). The people were pleased. But by the conclusion of Jesus' words, his listeners were "filled with rage" (4:28, NRSV). The story ends with their running him out of the city and trying to throw him over the edge of a cliff. What did Jesus say that turned the people around and made them so furious?

Well, according to Luke, he brought up two stories from the Hebrew Scriptures. The first story (from 1 Kings 17:8-16) is about the prophet Elijah. Elijah goes to a town in Sidon named Zarephath, where a widow lives with her son. It is a time of drought and the widow has only "a handful of meal in a jar" and "a little oil in a jug." Elijah instructs her to have no fear, to make him a little cake with the oil and meal, and then to make one for herself and her son. He promises that the Lord God of Israel, in this time of famine, will insure that the jar of meal and the jug of oil will not fail until the day the rain returned.

The second story Jesus told (from 2 Kings 5:1-14) is about the commander of the army of the King of Syria, Naaman, a man who had leprosy. At the advice of an Israelite slave girl, Naaman, with his horses and chariots, travels to the house of the prophet of Israel, Elisha, and asks to be healed. Elisha sends out a messenger to instruct Naaman to wash seven times in the Jordan. Naaman thinks this is ridiculous, but is eventually persuaded to do so. And he is healed.

Now why did Jesus' telling of these two miracle stories from the Hebrew Scriptures offend his listeners? Because they are stories of foreigners knowing God's help when Israel did not. "The truth is, there were many widows in Israel in the days of Elijah," Jesus says, but only a widow in Sidon was helped (Luke 4:24-26, NRSV). "There were also many lepers in Israel in the time of the prophet Elisha," says Jesus, "and none of them was cleansed except Naaman the Syrian" (4:27, NRSV). Jesus' message is clear. God's favor was not just for Jews, but for everyone.

Jesus' message was not unique to him. Hebrew prophets before had spoken of God's action in the lives of others, but it made people hostile. It is very human to want to enjoy special favor, to have special status, to be superior even. But Jesus reached out to all in his ministry. Jesus sought to open narrow minds, to expand notions of the holy. He angered people who sought to limit God, or who viewed their own faith as superior. God's interfaith agenda is an ancient one.

The interfaith movement for human unity has some parallels with the ecumenical movement for Christian unity. The ecumenical movement spanned the last century; indeed, the twentieth century was optimistically proclaimed "The Christian Century." An elaborate structure was put in place for the ecumenical movement, with local councils of churches, a National Council of Churches, and the World Council of Churches. As we enter the twenty-first century, the interfaith movement has no such elaborate structures. It lacks widespread support and funding.

I hope and pray that this will change, and signs are that it is changing. For building the interfaith movement, national networks like the North American Interfaith Network (*www.nain.org*); regional networks like the Interreligious Council of Central New York (*www.irccny.org*); and local networks that in many locations are called "ACT" or Area Congregations Together are beginning to make an impact.

Educational enterprises like The Pluralism Project at Harvard (*www.pluralism.org*) and The Center for Multifaith Education at Auburn Seminary in New York City (*www.auburnsem.org/multifaith*) are also making significant contributions. A new quarterly publication that is exciting to me is *Interreligious Insight: A journal of dialogue and engagement* (*www.interreligiousinsight.org*). *CrossCurrents*, a long-established journal published by The Association for Religion and Intellectual Life (*www.aril.org/crosscur.htm*), is another wonderful interfaith resource.

One of the most encouraging developments is the founding of the Interfaith Youth Core (*www.ifyc.org*). Eboo Patel, founder and executive director, is committed to building an interfaith youth movement.

I close with words from a contemporary hymn, "Won't You Let Me Be Your Servant?" Much sung and treasured in Christian churches, it might well resonate with people of all faiths, for it speaks to the human condition. It reminds me of God's call to engage in interfaith dialogue and cooperation.

We are pilgrims on a journey, we are travelers on the road;
We are here to help each other go the mile and bear the load.
I will hold the Christ-light for you in the shadow of your fear;
I will hold my hand out to you, speak the peace you long to hear.

The Servant Song by Richard Gillard
©1977 Scripture In Song (c/o Integrity Music)/ASCAP
c/o Integrity Music, Inc., 1000 Cody Road, Mobile, AL 36695

---

[1] Unpublished paper, "Beyond the Threefold Typology, Buddhist–Christian Monastic Dialogue." May 2004.

[2] Professor Bednarowski shared this at the opening of the Re-Imagining Conference of progressive Christian women held in Minneapolis in 1993.

[3] Transcribed by me from a tape recording of Professor Bednarowski's talk, "What It Means to Re-Imagine Together." The transcript was reviewed and approved by her July 26, 2005.

[4] Miriam Therese Winter, *Defecting in Place: Women Claiming Responsibility for Their Own Spiritual Lives*. New York: Crossroad, 1994.

[5] Letter dated June 19, 2004, sent for the Institute's opening celebration.

[6] Maura O'Neill, *Women Speaking, Women Listening: Women in Interreligious Dialogue (Faith Meets Faith Series)*. Maryknoll, New York: Orbis Books, 1990.

SECTION IV

WOMEN ENGAGED IN PEACEMAKING

*"May the world remember the women caught in wars not of
their making, remember women's dreams, and one day put into
action the power in women's knowledge."*

Fran Peavey[1]

To be alert to the activities of women who are activists for
peace and justice is to appreciate the wide variety of
approaches: there is no one method or mode to follow.
In peacemaking there is much room for diversity. Female or male,
each one of us is called to be effective in our own way, using our
own particular gifts, a point that Drew University professor Ed Long,
Jr. makes persuasively. Our task is to discover the uniqueness of our
role and to carry it out with as much dedication and skill as possible.
Long's words resonate with those of the apostle Paul:

Some people will find they can best work for peace by taking
part in campaigns and demonstrations. Others will find that
they can teach. Still others will find their best contribution to
come from analytical thinking and writing. Each needs the
others. Few can do all things well, and none has time to do
everything completely. It is of the very nature of peace to permit
different people to do different things toward its establishment, to stress different ways of making it real, to honor a
variety of gifts in the service of a common objective.[2]

In the pages that follow you will read about particular women
and the imaginative ways and means they have used and are using
to pursue peace. Their energy, fortitude, and courage can serve to
give us energy, fortitude, and courage—and to spark new ideas. To

113

set a stage for the accounts of women's initiatives, I turn to a poem of power and passion by Edna St. Vincent Millay (1892–1950). Here is "Conscientious Objector," first published in 1934.

> I shall die, but that is all that I shall do for Death.
> I hear him leading his horse out of the stall; I hear the clatter
>   on the barn-floor.
> He is in haste; he has business in Cuba, business in the
> Balkans, many calls to make this morning.
> But I will not hold the bridle while he cinches the girth.
> And he may mount by himself: I will not give him a leg up.
>
> Though he flick my shoulders with his whip, I will not tell
>   him which way the fox ran.
> With his hoof on my breast, I will not tell him where the
>   black boy hides in the swamp.
> I shall die, but that is all that I shall do for Death; I am not
>   on his pay-roll.
>
> I will not tell him the whereabouts of my friends nor of my
>   enemies either.
> Though he promise me much, I will not map him the route to
>   any man's door.
>
> Am I a spy in the land of the living, that I should deliver men
>   to Death?
> Brother, the password and the plans of our city are safe with
>   me; never through me
> Shall you be overcome.[3]

WOMEN PROMOTING PEACE

Queen Noor—Widow, Human Rights Activist, Philanthropist

When American Lisa Halaby, age twenty-six, made the decision to accept the proposal of King Hussein of Jordan to marry him in 1978, she made what she was later to call a "leap of faith." To read *Leap of Faith: Memoirs of an Unexpected Life*, a book about their love and life together (or to listen to it on tape, unabridged, as I did) is a rewarding experience. Here is an unusual perspective on political history and events in the Middle East, from an American woman of Arab descent, who as wife of a king became observer and partner at the highest level of international diplomacy. Especially interesting are the queen's accounts of her husband's strenuous and impassioned labors for peace in the deeply conflicted Middle East. No matter the disappointments, and there were many, he vigorously pursued peace until the time of his death in 1999. And Noor (the name given to her by King Hussein means "light" in Arabic) stood close by his side, offering encouragement and occasionally representing him and her adopted country, Jordan.

Queen Noor learned Arabic and converted to Islam, not because she had to (her husband never asked her to become a Muslim), but because she wanted to. Her description of what her new faith meant to her is moving:

My parents had not brought me up in any particular religion and had always encouraged me to choose my own spiritual path. The Muslim faith was the first religion I had been truly drawn to. I admired Islam's emphasis on a believer's direct relationship with God, the fundamental equality of rights of all men and women, and the reverence for the Prophet Muhammad as well as all the Prophets and messengers who came before him, since Adam, to Abraham, Moses, Jesus, and many others. Islam calls for fairness, tolerance, and charity: "Let there be no compulsion in religion," the Quran commands (2:256). And "Not one of you is a true believer until he desires for his brother what he desires for himself," reads one of the sayings of the Prophet Muhammad. I was attracted, too, by its simplicity and call for justice. Islam is a very personal belief system. There are prayer leaders and religious scholars but no intermediaries or bureaucrats, as in other monotheistic religions. No Muslim is better than any other Muslim except by piety. Honesty, faithfulness, and moderation are a few of the virtues that Islam calls for, and by which one Muslim can have merit over another.[4]

115

After becoming a Muslim, Queen Noor reports, she felt a sense of belonging to a larger community for the first time in her life. The faith became especially important after her husband died and she was left to carry on alone. Her description of making the haj, the pilgrimage to Mecca, gives insight into the spiritual power of this experience:

Above us on a hillside overlooking the main entrance to the [Great Mosque, the Masjid Al Haram Al Sharif], we saw the Hashimite fort that had belonged to Hussein's family—an ethereal golden stone structure that seemed to glow in the waning light of day and the loveliest building in Mecca after the mosque. Inside we joined a flowing river of humanity—men and women from all corners of the earth, alone or in groups, families and neighbors, all praying to God as Muslims have done since Prophet Muhammad's mission and revelation of the Quran....

As hours passed in prayer and reflection, I was imbued with a sense of gratitude for Hussein's extraordinary example—his faith, his patience and calm in the face of conflict and hostility, his vision of peace....

In our final months together, he taught me that there is power in acceptance, that the path to victory sometimes requires us to submit and trust and so to transcend....

I knew too that faith would sustain me in the days and months ahead, and that I would return to Mecca, *Insha'Allah*, to this living embodiment of Islam's timeless message—piety before God through truthfulness, humility, sacrifice, and empathy for one's fellow man.[5]

Today Queen Noor's stepson Abdullah is King of Jordan. Her four children live in places all over the globe and she divides her time between Jordan, Washington, D.C., and London. Her life is focused on the international stage as she seeks to make a difference, particularly in the lives of women. In October 2002, Queen Noor gave testimony in Washington, D.C., urging the United States to sign the Convention on the Elimination of All Forms of Discrimination Against Women (CEDAW). Jordan signed the treaty in 1992; the U.S. has yet to sign. "It is very frustrating that women's voices are only slowly increasing in numbers,"[6] Queen Noor laments.

A reporter from *Ms.* magazine who interviewed her for an article about "What is next for Queen Noor?" found her to be "a policy wonk"—a political and committed woman whose efforts are now largely directed to developing plans for an international leadership center and to the King Hussein Foundation. Continuing her efforts to build bridges between communities and cultures, Queen Noor writes:

King Hussein always emphasized that true peace is not created by treaties between governments, but must be built between people. And to bring people together, we had to begin with our children. The only way to overcome the enmity of previous generations is to enable the next generation, the future guardians of peace, to meet and interact openly and honestly in a secure atmosphere of trust. Education and exposure can impress upon young people the importance of resolving conflicts without violence, teach them the skills with which to do it, and to make their voices heard in issues that affect them. What if we today placed a premium on education for peace, a commitment to it equal to what previous generations devoted to military academies and combat readiness? We might well achieve a more lasting security than war could ever provide.[7]

Ann Madsen—Author

Ann Madsen has written *Making Their Own Peace*, a primer for peace illustrated by the lives of twelve women living in Jerusalem, "a city of perpetual war." The book tells of the courage and persistence of twelve extraordinary individuals—Muslims, Jews, and Christians— who view themselves as ordinary. Much of the narrative is in the words of the women themselves.

Over a thirty-year period of annual visits and a five-year residency while teaching in the Holy City, Madsen learned about the women and came to know and love them. Why, she wondered, do they stay, war after war? After all, they live with "terror as their neighbor, never knowing when a bus, a street, or a market… will explode around them." Madsen began to ask, and as she talked with women, she learned that of necessity they find strategies— personal, not political—for their own peace, as they continue to hope for peace.

Madsen writes: "These women have remembered or rediscovered that what may appear to be impossible can really be accomplished. They have lived the impossible."[8] She concludes:

> In this beleaguered city, whether at war or fighting for peace, they weren't waiting to see what would happen next. Each, in her own way, was working on the tiny interim miracles she could manage. If the big miracle of political peace material-ized, fine, but if it was perpetually postponed, surely more tiny miracles would surface in each of their lives and spread into wider and wider circles.[9]

One of the twelve women is Sahir Dajani, who has gone from village to village in the West Bank, working with Palestinian women to establish cooperatives and thus to empower them. Sahir and her husband have four children, now grown, and have lived most of their married lives in Jerusalem:

> My husband says, "God looks at what we do, how we think, and then He judges us. He doesn't judge you because you're a Muslim or a Christian." I agree with him.…
>
> You believe in the values of your religion. So you try to adapt it to your philosophy and whatever good you do. I begin with the good values of Islam. There are values in each religion. So you have to look at the good values and then live accordingly.[10]

Ruth Harriet Jacobs—Poet and Scholar

Ruth Jacobs, born in 1924, is a Quaker, a member of the Society of Friends, known for their opposition to war and violence. As a newspaper reporter, she "had a front seat" on World War II, and later she served as a volunteer with paraplegic and mentally scarred veterans. In 1991, Jacobs was enraged by the killing in the first Persian Gulf War and by the inability of political leaders to find a peaceful solution. She took citizen action—wrote letters, phoned, picketed, prayed, stood in silent vigils. Determined to "counter warpower with peacepower," she decided to collect and publish the words of people who hate war and work for peace.

Ruth Jacobs placed two tiny ads in magazines inviting antiwar, pro-peace contributions for an anthology. Her expectation was that hundreds of contributions might come in; instead she received almost three thousand. Over a period of some four months her standard size, RFD outdoor mailbox was filled tight; and Ruth began to be concerned about her mail deliverer's back! Offerings came from all fifty states and from people of all ages and occupations. The hardest part for Ruth was culling the collection and making decisions about what to publish. "It was agony to turn down some fine writing and thinking because of lack of space, the need for diversity, and the desire to make as many nonrepetitive points." She wrote thank-you letters to all and sent "the longest rejection slip on record," urging people to publish elsewhere. To save space, she eliminated her own poems. *We Speak for Peace*, a thick paperback book, was published in 1993. Here is just one of its many remarkable offerings—"Peacework," by Elsie Bowman Kurtz[11]:

> They call it a summit meeting,
> but it is really a quilting party.
> They sit around the table
> carefully stitching together
> little squares of peace.
> Every piece a different fabric,
> colors harmonizing or clashing,
> endless variety of designs,
> difficult to fit
> into a pattern.
> It is tedious work,
> smoothing wrinkles,

hemming ragged edges,
trimming loose threads,
attending to details
with tiny invisible stitches,
to make a patchwork quilt
that will warm the world.

Margo Ramlal-Nankoe—Professor of Sociology

I first learned about Margo Ramlal-Nankoe from an Ithaca College senior, Bernadette Johnston, who asked me in an e-mail message to participate in a vigil (held in April, 2004):

> I am writing to you because of a project my Honors in Sociology class is working on. We are planning a display on the academic quad to honor the lives lost in the war on Iraq. This includes all lives, all human beings, not just Americans (but including Americans). We will be sticking around 14,000 chopsticks (even though the death count is higher now) in the ground to symbolize all of those who have died in the Iraq war....
>
> This vigil is a peaceful coming together in hope for the future and to honor those who have given their lives (willingly or unwillingly). We will have students playing instruments and people singing as well as lighting candles. Your presence and that of other professors and chaplains will be very meaningful. If you are not comfortable speaking, we would love to have you there just to share your presence. Let me know what you think.

I responded that I thought this was a terrific idea and of course I would be there that night. As it turned out, I felt so overcome by emotion that the only words I spoke were words of thanks to those who did speak. Students told wrenching, personal stories of family members killed or suffering. Supported by one another, they found the courage to share their pain, publicly, for the first time. Until then, I had no idea how deeply the violence of the war in Iraq had penetrated our own tranquil campus. In the candlelight there were tears and long hugs.

Afterward I e-mailed Bernadette to thank her for her part in organizing the unusual lawn display and vigil, to remark on the speakers, and to ask her about the woman professor standing in the background. Bernadette replied:

> The professor is Margo Ramlal-Nankoe. She is a sociology pro-
> fessor and teaches mostly classes on race and ethnic global
> issues. She wanted us to do a project... and share it with the
> school.... We thought of the display (kind of in response to the
> IC Republican display of American flags that symbolized all of
> the allied deaths). We thought that all loss of life should be rep-
> resented, because that is the reality of war. At any rate, Margo is
> an amazing intellectual and human being. You should meet her!

I did meet Margo. I learned that she is the person who inspired students to form Students for a Just Peace (SJP) on campus, a group that wants to bring peace in Israel/Palestine. From the Dutch West Indies, Margo has a mixed religious heritage—Hindu/Christian/ Muslim. She has the gift of teaching and uses it to motivate and encourage the imagination and creativity of young people. Her values have clearly influenced her own daughter, who works with the United Nations; and after the devastating tsunami of December 26, 2004, she was assigned to the territory of Aceh on the island of Sumatra, Indonesia.

Kim Hines and Marina Hoshi—Mothers and Educators

Kim Hines, born in Chicago in 1965, and Marina Hoshi, born in Tokyo in 1963, met in Hawaii in 2000, where both were living with their husbands and children. After 9/11 they founded a nonprofit organization known as WorldMAP, or World Mothers Acting for Peace. The entrepreneurial founders are dedicated to "amplifying the maternal voice of peace." They are "demanding nonviolent solutions to world conflicts for the sake of every mother's child." Kim and Marina know that our own children's well-being "depends on the well-being of all children, regardless of their location on Earth." On their Web site they present resources for Moms as peace activists, as well as ideas for teaching children the power of non-violent solutions. World Mothers Acting for Peace can be found on the Web at *www.peacemothers.homestead.com.*

Mothers working for peace is not new. The guiding spirit behind Mother's Day was Julia Ward Howe, a woman who had six children (four lived to adulthood) and was passionate about peace. In the first Mother's Day proclamation made in Boston in 1870, Howe exhorted:

Arise, then, women of this day!

Arise all women who have hearts, whether your baptism be of water or of fears!

Say firmly: "We will not have great questions decided by irrelevant agencies,

"Our husbands shall not come to us reeking with carnage, for caresses and applause.

"Our sons shall not be taken from us to unlearn all that we have been able to teach them of charity, mercy, and patience.

"We women of one country will be too tender of those of another country to allow our sons to be trained to injure theirs."

From the bosom of a devastated Earth a voice goes up with our own. It says, "Disarm! Disarm!"

The sword of murder is not the balance of justice! Blood does not wipe out dishonor nor violence indicate possession.

As men have often forsaken the plow and the anvil at the summons of war, let women now leave all that may be left of home for a great and earnest day of counsel.

Let them meet first, as women, to bewail and commemorate the dead.

Let them then solemnly take counsel with each other as the means whereby the great human family can live in peace,

And each bearing after her own time the sacred impress, not of Caesar, but of God.

In the name of womanhood and humanity, I earnestly ask that a general congress of women without limit of nationality be appointed and held at some place deemed most convenient and at the earliest period consistent with its object, to promote the alliance of the different nationalities, the amicable settlement of international questions, the great and general interests of peace.[12]

MAKING CONNECTIONS THROUGH THE INTERNET— WOMEN'S PEACE PROJECTS

The most efficient tool for identifying, locating, and connecting with women's peace organizations—international, national, and even regional and local—is the Internet. With the assistance of search engines and links, turning to the World Wide Web will quickly help one discover countless opportunities for peace work. This amazing technology is new in my lifetime, but my young college students have not known a world without it. It has the capacity to empower peace activists in a way that I am willing to call a godsend. By networking through the Internet, we can collaborate and be effective as never before. I briefly describe just two international women's organizations that might serve as entry points.

Women's International League for Peace and Freedom (WILPF)
www.wilpf.org

The Women's International League for Peace and Freedom is the oldest women's peace organization in the world. It was founded in April 1915 in The Hague, the Netherlands by some thirteen hundred women from Europe and North America. Coming from countries engaged in fighting each other in a world war, they protested the killings and destruction, proposed ways to end it and to prevent war in the future. The co-founders (as noted in my introduction to Section III) were Jane Addams and Emily Greene Balch. Today WILPF is an international organization with national sections in

123

thirty-seven countries, covering all continents. Its International Secretariat is based in Geneva with a New York United Nations office (see *www.wilpf.int.ch*).

Nearly a century after this NGO's[13] founding, the vision of WILPF has not changed, for contemporary members understand, as did their foremothers, that for peace to flourish, more is involved than treaties and a turning away of weapons. True peace cannot exist under systems of exploitation. Challenges of the twenty-first century are identified:

- The equality of all people is a world free of sexism, racism, classism, and homophobia,
- The guarantee of fundamental human rights including the right to sustainable development,
- An end to all forms of violence: rape, battering, exploitation, intervention and war,
- The transfer of world resources from military to human needs, leading to economic justice within and among nations, and
- World disarmament and peaceful resolution of international conflicts via the United Nations

Women in Black *www.womeninblack.org*

Women in Black is not an organization, but an international peace network. It is a means of mobilization and a formula for action. Women in Black stand in silent vigil to protest war. "Our silence is visible," they say. "We wear black as a symbol of sorrow for all victims of war, for the destruction of people, nature and the fabric of life."

Vigils were started in Israel in 1988 by women protesting against Israel's occupation of the West Bank and Gaza and have since developed in countries around the world—Italy, Spain, Germany, England, Azerbaijan, Columbia, etc. Women in Black in Belgrade was formed in 1991 and they have been opposing nationalist aggression ever since. In a 1995 publication they wrote:

We are still, after three and a half years, in the streets of Belgrade. When it rains, when the city is chained by frost, when the summer heat simmers, and when we rejoice in the spring flowering, and when the autumn brings sadness...

Sometimes there are only a few of us. But we know that those who are not present, those who are physically unable to come, are with us. And to tell the truth when there are more of us it is not so easy to remain silent while we are standing. We whisper to encourage and support each other, especially when we are exposed to insults. We rebuke each other when the whispering turns into a racket. Although it is not easy to find new ways and codes of feminine hostility to war, we have kept the "ritual" of black and silence.[14]

Women in Black have received awards locally and internationally in recognition of their work for peace. This ever-expanding network invites women to stand with them. United Methodist Women National Seminar participants in 2003 stood as Women in Black in Nashville to advocate for peace.

Recently, I found another wonderful reference to this group. Anne Lamott, author of the runaway best-seller *Traveling Mercies*, describes a San Francisco peace march that she participated in:

The energy and signs and faces of the crowd were an intoxicating balm, and by some marvelous yogic stretch, we all stopped trying to figure out whom and what we agreed with, and who the bad elements were.... You just had to let go, because Market Street was wide enough for us all, and we began to march, each a small part of one big body, fascinatingly out of control, like protoplasm bobbing along....

The Women in Black moved solemnly in the middle of the throng, steadfast and profound, witnessing for peace. They dressed in black, like the Madres in South America. They stopped you with their presence, like punctuation, made you remember why you were there.[15]

THINK GLOBALLY, ACT LOCALLY

In their villages, hometowns, and cities the world over, women are choosing life. They are resisting all that is death-dealing and working for that which is life-giving. While thinking globally, they are acting locally for peace and justice. As a kind of illustrative case study, I close by telling about just a few of the many peace and justice initiatives in the Finger Lakes region of upstate New York, where I live.

Seeds of Peace *www.1to1peaceproject.org*

The notion that peace must be nurtured for it to grow has given rise to many grassroots "seeds of peace" initiatives. In Waterloo, New York, Karen Burns has started "Seeds of Peace." Its Web site provides a click-and-print worksheet consisting of "seeds," or one-word messages ("peace," "understanding," "love," and "kindness"), that are to be colored and cut out. A second worksheet is a click-and-print envelope that is to be colored, cut, folded, sealed, and addressed. By putting the "seeds" into the envelope and sending it, one creates one's own message of peace. Suggested options include: adding a photo of oneself; adding a drawing of something one loves; adding a personal message; and asking for a return note.

This is a project that can be done in a group—with family, friends, at club meetings or religious organizations. Messages can be sent to anyone—government leaders and representatives, schools, hospitals, sister-city projects, peace organizations, and so on. The idea of reaching out to one another and making connections comes from Karen's conviction that the people of this world are peace loving and do not want war.

The late John Wallach founded a different "Seeds of Peace" project in 1993 (after the first attack on the World Trade Center). In this nonprofit, U.S.-based, international organization, teenagers are the "Seeds." From the first summer when Israeli, Palestinian, and Egyptian youth met at an international summer camp in Maine, the program has grown tremendously. For a full history and more information, see *www.seedsofpeace.org*.

Women Transcending Boundaries *www.wtb.org*

"Bringing women of faith together after 9/11" is what the Women Transcending Boundaries (WTB) Web site says. And that's how the organization began, in Syracuse, New York, when two women— one a Christian, one a Muslim—got together for a cup of coffee. Betsy Wiggins invited Danya Wellmon, from the *masjid* (the Islamic Society of Central New York) to her home to find out what she might do to be of help. Out of their conversation remarkable things happened. A few more women came to the next meeting, and then more, and still more, until the group outgrew Betsy's home and the venue needed to be changed. Their vision was compelling and many were eager to join in:

> We are an egalitarian community of women coming together to respect and learn more about each other's various spiritual beliefs and common concerns. It is our intent to share our experiences with the wider community, to educate and to serve.[16]

After *The New York Times* ran an article about the organization in March, 2003, Betsy and Danya began fielding inquires from around the country. Calls came from CNN, Oprah Winfrey, *Family Circle* magazine, and others wanting to know more and to tell their story. As part of its anniversary coverage of the tragedies of September 11, in 2003 CNN International showed news segments about Women Transcending Boundaries and its impact on Muslim women. *O, The Oprah Magazine* included WTB in a feature on the power of women's groups across the nation in its November 2003 issue, and that same month *Family Circle* interviewed Betsy Wiggins. She was quoted:

> Through the group, I've learned what a single person can do. If I hadn't made that first call, I might have gone on feeling helpless and afraid. But I did call, and the result is that I've made friends for life, and together we are making a difference.[17]

Women's Interfaith Institute *www.womensinterfaithinstitute.org*

Women leaders in the regional organizations mentioned above understand that the best way to make a difference is to work together. By cooperating with one another, by networking, by sharing information, we maximize our effectiveness. None of us wants to go it alone, or to compete, but we want to encourage and support one another's best efforts. And this is just what we are doing. For a description of our organization and peace initiatives, please see Chapter 11.

---

[1] *I Remember/Sjeçam Se: Writings by Bosnian Women Refugees*, Fran Peavey, U.S. editor. San Francisco: Aunt Lute Books, 1996, n.p.

[2] Edward Leroy Long, Jr., *Peace Thinking in a Warring World*. Philadelphia: The Westminster Press, 1983, pp. 98-99.

[3] *Edna St. Vincent Millay: Selected Poems*. Colin Falck, ed. New York: HarperPerennial, 1992, p. 103.

[4] Queen Noor, *Leap of Faith: Memoirs of an Unexpected Life*. New York: Miramax Books, 2003, p. 96.

[5] Ibid., pp. 437-439.

[6] Elaine Lafferty, "Queen Noor, The Next Chapter," *Ms.*, Fall 2003, pp. 38-39.

[7] Noor, p. 385.

[8] Ann N. Madsen, *Making Their Own Peace: Twelve Women of Jerusalem*. New York: Lantern Books, 2003, p. 8.

[9] Ibid., p. 255.

[10] Ibid., pp. 169-170.

[11] *We Speak for Peace: An Anthology*, Ruth Harriet Jacobs, ed. Manchester, Connecticut: Knowledge, Ideas & Trends, Inc., 1993, p. 292.

[12] "Mother's Day Proclamation 1870," by Julia Ward Howe.

[13] An "NGO" is a Non-Governmental Organization. The term is a common one, used frequently to refer to organizations in the nonprofit world. WILPF is one of the many NGOs that have consultative status at the UN.

[14] *I Remember/Sjeçam Se*, n.p.

[15] Anne Lamott, "Market Street," in *Plan B: Further Thoughts on Faith*. New York: Riverhead Books, 2005, pp. 316, 318.

[16] From the Web site of Women Transcending Boundaries, *www.wtb.org*.

[17] Ibid.

LET PEACE BEGIN WITH ME—
CONTEMPLATIVE PRAYER
AND INNER PEACE

Grant us to seek peace where it is truly found!
In your will, O God, is our peace!

Prayer of Father Thomas Merton, 1962[1]

For persons of faith whose usual mode of being is action, the importance and value of meditation or contemplative prayer is not always acknowledged, appreciated, or experienced. Because college and university chaplains are both positioned to respond to interest in spirituality among youth and society and prone to focus on action rather than the inner life, leaders at the Garrison Institute in Garrison, New York, organized a symposium for their benefit. The working premise was that "contemplative practices have historically been a key means for effecting the inner transformation that leads to genuine and positive transformation in the world."[2] This multifaith gathering focused on contemplative practices in four religious traditions: Judaism, Christianity, Islam, and Buddhism. Michael Faber, the Jewish chaplain at Ithaca College, and I attended together, both of us delighted to be able to take advantage of an unusual offering.

The widely known author and Cistercian "Trappist" monk who addressed the Christian practice of contemplative prayer at our symposium was Father Thomas Keating. He made the claim, startling to me, that if a Christian preacher does not take time out for centering prayer, then that person is not preaching the Gospel. To preach the good news aright, Keating insisted, is to do as Jesus did and regularly withdraw into solitude. Jesus drew apart from the crowds to renew and refresh his spirit. By choosing to do the same, to set aside time for daily contemplative prayer or meditation (the two words were used interchangeably at this symposium), we ground ourselves in the Spirit of Life and Love and experience the peace of God that passes all human understanding.

I must admit that I arrived in Garrison weighed down with a Things-to-Do list for our free time, a canvas bag of correspondence, and my laptop computer. After listening to Father Keating, it took me about thirty seconds to figure out that if I were to use any retreat time to catch up on work, I would be subverting the symposium's purpose. So I set aside my To-Do list, sat still during periods of unscheduled time, breathing deeply, relaxed, and opened my soul to the moment. Per instructions, I did not try to suppress my thoughts, but allowed them to flow freely.

Three days later I left having accomplished "nothing," but feeling stress free and at peace. In other words, I had experienced what planners had hoped I would experience—their point being that those engaged in peace and social justice work must come from a place of inner peace if they are to have energy for the long haul. I thought of a saying attributed to Gandhi, "You must be the change you want to see in the world," and decided, "You must be the *peace* you want to see in the world."

That I had this experience of inner peace in a multifaith gathering is notable. I learned that the practice of meditation or contemplative prayer has the power to transcend boundaries that divide. It can bring diverse peoples together and create a spirit of harmony, unity, and peace. When I was pastor of a church in the Berkshire Hills of western Massachusetts, Andrew Warner, our student intern from the Harvard Divinity School, described to me how he had started a weekly, interfaith prayer gathering at school. People sat for about an hour, he explained, in silence. Prayers were not spoken aloud. At the time I didn't get it: how would sitting together without speaking help people of different faiths come to a better understanding of one another? This did not seem to me to be a very effective practice for promoting the interfaith project. My experience of contemplative prayer in the interfaith setting at the Garrison Institute leads me to confess that I did not properly appreciate the value of Andrew's initiative. I now recognize that not only is contemplative prayer in community an important practice in and of itself but also it can be an important beginning step toward interfaith worship/liturgy.

Rarely do all the elements come together that allow us to share worship with faithful people of other religions, but when that happens it is particularly exhilarating. Bodies, hearts, minds, and souls experience sisterhood and brotherhood through carefully designed, interfaith liturgies that do not deny our differences, disagreements, or historical clashes, but do express our human unity under God.

While the events of 9/11 were horrific, they were the occasion of the extraordinary coming together of people in interfaith services to pray and remember those who died. My friend Pat Patterson, a founding member of the Women's Interfaith Institute in the Berkshires and study guide author, told me about a service in Claremont, California, which she attended. People gathered on the evening of September 13 for "An Interfaith Service of Prayer for the Nation and World." It was sponsored by the Claremont Ecumenical Council. Divided into sections, the service moved through a deeply moving process of reflection and petition:

In Preparation for Prayer
In Prayer for the Human Family,
In Prayer for Comfort,
In Prayer for our Nation in Crisis,
In Prayer for our Enemies,
In Prayer for the World and Peace,
In Prayer and Community.

Included were prayers from the Jewish, Christian, and Muslim traditions. Jews, Muslims, Catholics, Protestants, Quakers, and Mormons were present and gave leadership. The service concluded with singing "This Is My Song" to the beautiful tune Finlandia. The second stanza is:

> My country's skies are bluer than the ocean,
>   and sunlight beams on cloverleaf and pine;
> but other lands have sunlight, too, and clover,
>   and skies are everywhere as blue as mine.
> O hear my song, thou God of all the nations,
>   a song of peace for their land and for mine.[3]

The bulletin gave suggestions on how to give blood through the Red Cross or donate funds through Church World Service.

Pat remembers, "It was a truly memorable evening unparalleled in our community's experience. We were of one broken heart, yearning for peace and understanding. The evening opened up dialogue and friendship, especially with people in the Muslim community who had been almost invisible to us before."

Thanksgiving, Martin Luther King, Jr. Day, and Earth Day are annual occasions for creating interfaith liturgies. To work with women of different faith traditions to prepare a liturgy can be incredibly rewarding. In 1987, Norma U. Levitt, president of the World Conference on Religion and Peace, described the experience of Protestant, Roman Catholic, and Jew preparing an interreligious worship service, an experience that brought "understanding, creativity, and enjoyment." She writes in *Women of Faith in Dialogue*:

> The hours spent together by the small planning committee had built mutual acceptance of individual differences and each person's rich spiritual resources. Because of this slow building of trust and appreciation, the process of creation remained open until the last moment.[4]

Church Women United (CWU) is one organization that has been introducing interfaith worship into traditional settings. During CWU World Community Day in November 2002, the theme of interfaith worship was "Daughters of Abraham Called to Peace" and in November 2004, the interfaith theme was "In Faith, Women

Shape the Future for Peace." The World Community Day 2006 interfaith worship service was created by members of the Women's Interfaith Institute. Its theme is "Signs of the Times—Signs of Healing." More pioneering initiatives like these are sure to foster connection, break down barriers that keep us apart, and lead to reconciliation.

"Let there be peace on earth, and let it begin with me," are the opening words of a popular song by Sy Miller and Jill Jackson sometimes used in interfaith services. It is the song used by Rotary International, something I learned in 2005 at a celebration of the service organization's one-hundredth anniversary.

Let peace begin with me; let this be the moment now.

With every step I take, let this be my solemn vow:

to take each moment and live each moment in peace eternally.

Let there be peace on earth, and let it begin with me.[5]

Personal efforts toward peacemaking are discouraging when day after day reports from flashpoints around the globe bring news of violence, destruction, and unspeakable human suffering. "What possible difference am I making?" you and I are likely to wonder. We need regular encouragement for the work ever before us. Support comes from networking with other peacemakers. Hope comes from a power greater than ourselves.

Whichever faith tradition we embrace, in the practice of contemplative prayer, we connect with this hope. We come to a place of trust where we can turn it over. However bleak the world situation appears, however elusive true human community, we give it our best, then let go and let God. The contemporary prophet William Sloane Coffin assures us that "God is not mocked, and the kingdom of God comes through God's judgment, which promises the eventual downfall of every other kind of kingdom."[6] In faith, we know that this is so. In the will of the One God is our peace.

I conclude with a memory of forty years ago and a prayer for the future. In 1964, I was a new bride living in Istanbul, Turkey, with my husband. He was teaching at the American College for Girls, sister school to Robert College (founded by American Congregationalist missionaries), and we had a faculty apartment overlooking the stunningly beautiful Bosporus. A vivid recollection of that time is the exotic and strangely haunting sound of muezzins calling worshipers to prayer. I was young then, I did not understand Arabic, and my spiritual life was so narrowly Christian that I did not connect with those invitations to prayer. Rather, what the sounds signaled to me was, this place is different, *really* different. It sure isn't Europe.

Now as I dream of an opportunity to return to Istanbul, I imagine that in my maturity I might hear the muezzins' call quite differently, indeed for what it is—not as exotic, background sound, but as a call to centering prayer:

Allahu Akbar! God is most great! God is most great! God is most great! I bear witness that there is no god but Allah! I bear witness that there is no god but Allah! I testify that Mohammed is the apostle of Allah! Come to prayer! Come to prayer! Come to prosperity! Come to prosperity! God is most great! God is most great! There is no god but Allah![7]

I think now what a blessing it would be to be reminded several times a day to pray, to be reminded several times a day that God is great and that there is no god but God, to feel connected through prayer to my Muslim sisters and brothers, to celebrate not only the oneness of God, but the oneness of human life.

Carol Zaleski, a professor of religion at Smith College, has expressed a similar thought about the Muslim call to prayer in her reflections on a controversy in an urban community near Detroit. Opposition came from some residents of Hamtramck when the city council voted unanimously to amend a noise ordinance so that one of the mosques can broadcast, five times a day, by loudspeaker, the call to prayer. In "Taking Time Out for Allah," Zaleski writes, "It may not be a bad thing to be roused five times a day by the praise of God, even in an unfamiliar tongue. Better still if another faith's call to prayer prompts us to recover Christian practices that have suffered neglect."[8]

In recalling such Christian practices now neglected, one might think of Jean Francois Millet's well-loved painting of "The Angelus," which hangs in the Louvre in Paris. Here a peasant couple has stopped work in a field to bow in prayer at the sound of the distant church bell. In this Roman Catholic form of devotion, the Angelus bell rings to call people to prayer morning, noon, and evening.

In closing, I want to leave you with a prayer we recite at the Women's Interfaith Institute. I do not know the source, but I am confident that whoever first offered it is glad for her prayer to be shared and lovingly used.

> *Creator of the World, Our God, Adonai, Allah, the Compassionate One, Wisdom, Spirit: we call you by many names for you have made us many people. May this day be a blessing to us. May the breath of the Spirit fill our hearts, replenish our spirits, and inspire us in our journey together.*
> *Amen.*

---

[1] Thomas Merton, *Passion for Peace: The Social Essays*, William H. Shannon, ed. New York: Crossroad, 1995, p. 329.

[2] The symposium was held in February, 2004 and reported in the first issue of the Garrison Institute Newsletter, P.O. Box 532, Garrison, New York 10524, Summer 2004, p. 7. A second, similar event at the Garrison Institute occurred in April, 2005.

[3] *The United Methodist Hymnal*, Nashville: The United Methodist Publishing House, 1989, no. 437.

[4] *Women of Faith in Dialogue*, Virginia Ramey Mollenkott, ed. New York: Crossroad, 1990, p 183. This book includes not only Levitt's story of crafting an interreligious worship service but also the text of the service.

[5] *The United Methodist Hymnal*, no. 431.

[6] William Sloane Coffin, *Credo*. Louisville: Westminster John Knox Press, 2004, p. 97.

[7] Murray T. Titus, *The Young Moslem Looks at Life*. New York: Friendship Press, 1937, pp. 64-65.

[8] "Time Out for Allah," Carol Zaleski, *The Christian Century*, June 15, 2004, p. 37.

THE TENT OF ABRAHAM, HAGAR, & SARAH: A CALL FOR PEACEMAKING

"A Call for Peacemaking" appeared as a full-page advertisement in *The New York Times* on January 14, 2005, page A11. Months earlier Rabbi Arthur Waskow, director of the Shalom Center in Philadelphia, had used the Internet to circulate a statement on peacemaking and to invite Muslims, Christians, and Jews to be signatories to it. Waskow was joined in this appeal by Sister Joan Chittister, OSB, former president of the Leadership Conference of Women Religious; the Reverend Bob Edgar, general secretary of the National Council of Churches; and Dr. Sayyid Muhammad Syeed, general secretary of the Islamic Society of North America.[1] When the ad appeared, many leaders in all three religions had signed it.

A CALL FOR PEACEMAKING

We are members of the families of Abraham—Muslims, Christians, Jews.

Our traditions teach us to have compassion, seek justice, and pursue peace for all peoples. We bear especially deep concern for the region where Abraham grew and learned, taught and flourished. Today that region stretches from Iraq, where Abraham grew up, to Israel and Palestine, where he sojourned, and to Mecca and Egypt, where he visited.

Today our hearts are broken by the violence poured out upon the peoples of that broad region.

That violence has included terrorist attacks on and kidnappings of Americans, Israelis, Iraqis, Europeans, and others by various Palestinian and Iraqi groups and by Al Qaeda; the occupation of Palestinian lands by Israel and of Iraq by the United States; and the torture of prisoners by several different police forces, military forces, and governments in the region.

From our heartbreak at these destructive actions, we intend to open our hearts more fully to each other and to the suffering of all peoples.

In the name of the One God Whom we all serve and celebrate, we condemn all these forms of violence. To end the present wars and to take serious steps toward the peace that all our traditions demand of us, we call on governments and on the leaders of all religious and cultural communities to act.

We urge the US government to set a firm and speedy date for completing the safe return home from Iraq of all American soldiers and civilians under military contract. We urge the UN to work directly with Iraqi political groupings to transfer power in Iraq to an elected government.

We urge the UN, the US, the European Union, and Russia to convene a comprehensive peace conference through which the governments of Israel, the Palestinian Authority, Iran, and all Arab states conclude a full diplomatic, economic, and cultural peace with Israel and Palestine, defined approximately on the 1967 boundaries, with small mutual adjustments.

We urge the international community to work out lawful and effective means to deal with the dangers of international terrorism, the spread of nuclear and similar weapons, and conflicts over the control of oil and water.

We ourselves will act to create transnational and interfaith networks of Jews, Christians, and Muslims who will covenant together—

- to insist that governments take these steps,

- to undertake whatever nonviolent actions are necessary to prevent more violence and achieve a just peace throughout the region,

- and to grow grass-roots relationships that bind together those who have been enemies into a Compassionate Coalition.

According to tradition, Abraham, Hagar, and Sarah kept their tent open in all four directions, the more easily to share their food and water with travelers from anywhere. Like them, we welcome all who thirst and hunger for justice, peace, and dignity, to join in affirming this statement.[2]

---

[1] E-mail message from The Shalom Center on June 27, 2004. The Shalom Center is located at 6711 Lincoln Drive, Philadelphia, Pennsylvania 19119. *www.shalomctr.org*

[2] "A Call for Peacemaking," *The New York Times*, January 14, 2005, p. A11.

BIBLIOGRAPHY

Abdalati, Hammudah. *Islam in Focus.* Plainfield, Indiana: American Trust Publications, 1996.

Abrams, Irwin, ed. *The Words of Peace: Selections from the Speeches of the Winners of the Nobel Peace Prize.* New York: Newmarket Press, 1990.

Addams, Jane. "Newer Ideal of Peace," in *The Power of Nonviolence: Writings by Advocates of Peace,* Howard Zinn, introduction. Boston: Beacon Press, 2002, pp. 39–41.

Ahmed, Akbar S. *Islam Today: A Short Introduction to the Muslim World.* New York: I.B. Tauris Publishers, 2002.

Ali, Maulana Muhammad. *The Holy Qur'an: Arabic Text with English Translation and Commentary.* Dublin, Ohio: Ahmadiyya Anjuman Isha'at Islam Lahore Inc., USA, 2002.

Ambrogi, Thomas E. "A New Europe at Normandy" in *Fellowship,* published by the Fellowship of Reconciliation, November–December 2004. *www.forusa.org/fellowship/nov-dec-04/ambrogi.html*

Angelou, Maya. *On the Pulse of Morning.* New York: Random House, 1993.

Annan, Kofi. "Do We Still Have Universal Values?" *Interreligious Insight: A journal of dialogue and engagement.* Vol. 2, no. 3, July 2004, pp. 10–15.

Ariarajah, S. Wesley. "Do Christians and Muslims worship the same God?" *The Christian Century,* June 1, 2004, pp. 29–30.

Armstrong, Karen. *Holy War: The Crusades and Their Impact on Today's World.* New York: Anchor Books, 2001.

_____. *Muhammad: A Biography of the Prophet.* HarperSanFrancisco, 1993.

Bawer, Bruce. *Stealing Jesus: How Fundamentalism Betrays Christianity.* New York: Three Rivers Press, 1997.

Bhasin, Kamla, Smitu Kothari, and Bindia Thapar. *Voices of Sanity: Reaching Out for Peace.* New York: Apex Press, 2001.

Boulding, Elise. *Cultures of Peace: The Hidden Side of History.* Syracuse, New York: Syracuse University Press, 2000.

Cahill, Lisa Sowle. *Love Your Enemies: Discipleship, Pacifism, and Just War Theory.* Minneapolis: Fortress Press, 1994.

Carroll, James. *Crusade: Chronicles of an Unjust War.* New York: Metropolitan Books, 2004.

Carter, Jimmy. *Our Endangered Values, America's Moral Crisis.* New York: Simon & Schuster, 2005.

Castelli, Jim. *The Bishops and the Bomb: Waging Peace in a Nuclear Age.* Garden City, New York: Doubleday & Co., Inc., 1983.

Cejka, Mary Ann and Thomas Bamat. *Artisans of Peace: Grassroots Peacemaking among Christian Communities.* Maryknoll, New York: Orbis Books, 2003.

Coffin, William Sloane. *Credo.* Louisville: Westminster John Knox Press, 2004.

Coogan, Michael D., ed. *The New Oxford Annotated Bible: New Revised Standard Version.* Third edition. New York: Oxford University Press, 2001.

Eck, Diana. "Difference Is No Excuse for Hatred," *Voices of the Religious Left: A Contemporary Sourcebook,* Rebecca T. Alpert, ed. Philadelphia: Temple University Press, 2000, pp. 261-264.

_____. *Encountering God: A Spiritual Journey from Bozeman to Banaras.* Boston: Beacon Press, 1993.

_____. *A New Religious America: How a "Christian Country" Has Become the World's Most Religiously Diverse Nation.* HarperSanFrancisco, 2001.

Esposito, John L. *Islam: The Straight Path.* New York: Oxford University Press, 1998.

Falck, Colin, ed. *Edna St. Vincent Millay: Selected Poems.* New York: HarperPerennial, 1992.

Feiler, Bruce. *Abraham: A Journey to the Heart of Three Faiths.* New York: HarperCollins, 2002.

Fisher, Mary Pat and Lee W. Bailey. *An Anthology of Living Religions.* Upper Saddle River, New Jersey: Prentice Hall, 2000.

Galley, Howard E. *The Ceremonies of the Eucharist.* Cambridge, Massachusetts: Cowley Publications, 1989.

Gates, David. "The Pop Prophets," *Newsweek.* May 24, 2004, pp. 45-47.

Gilligan, James. *Violence: Our Deadly Epidemic and Its Causes.* New York: G. P. Putnam's Sons, 1996.

Gopin, Marc. *Holy War, Holy Peace: How Religion Can Bring Peace to the Middle East.* New York: Oxford University Press, 2002.

Griffith, Elisabeth. *In Her Own Right: The Life of Elizabeth Cady Stanton.* New York: Oxford University Press, 1984.

Griffith, Lee. *The War on Terrorism and the Terror of God.* Grand Rapids, Michigan: William B. Eerdmans Publishing Co., 2002

Gwin, Larry. *Baptism: A Vietnam Memoir.* New York: Ivy Books, 1999.

Hedges, Chris. *War Is a Force That Gives Us Meaning.* New York: Anchor Books, 2003.

Hersh, Seymour M. *Chain of Command: The Road from 9/11 to Abu Ghraib.* New York: HarperCollins Publishers, 2004.

Hillman, James. *A Terrible Love of War.* New York: Penguin Books, 2004.

Hitt, William. *A Global Ethic: The Leadership Challenge.* Columbus, Ohio: Battelle Press, 1996.

Hunt, Helen LaKelly. *Faith and Feminism, A Holy Alliance.* New York: Atria Books, 2004.

Horsley, Richard A. *Jesus and Empire.* Minneapolis: Fortress Press, 2003.

Jacobs, Ruth Harriet, ed. *We Speak for Peace: An Anthology.* Manchester, Connecticut: Knowledge, Ideas & Trends, Inc., 1993.

The Jewish Publication Society. *TANAKH: The New JPS Translation According to the Traditional Hebrew Text.* Philadelphia: The Jewish Publication Society, 1985.

Juergensmeyer, Mark. *Terror in the Mind of God: The Global Rise of Religious Violence.* University of California Press, 2003.

Kearney, John. "My God Is Your God," Op-Ed, *The New York Times,* January 28, 2004, n.p.

Kennedy, John F. "The Peace Corps" and "The Strategy of Peace" in Theodore C. Sorensen, ed. *"Let the Word Go Forth," The Speeches, Statements, and Writings of John F. Kennedy, 1947–1963.* New York: Delacorte Press, 1988, pp. 60-61 and 282-290.

King, Ursula. "Feminism: the Missing Dimension in the Dialogue of Religions," in *Pluralism and the Religions,* John D'Arcy May, ed. Herndon, Virginia: Cassell, 1998.

Kireopoulos, Antonios, ed. *For the Peace of the World.* New York: Friendship Press, 2006.

Knitter, Paul F. *One Earth Many Religions: Multifaith Dialogue & Global Responsibility.* Maryknoll, New York: Orbis Books, 1995.

Kristof, Nicholas D. "Jesus and Jihad," *The New York Times,* July 17, 2004, p. A13.

Lafferty, Elaine. "Queen Noor, the Next Chapter." *Ms.,* Fall 2003, pp. 32-39.

LaHaye, Tim and Jerry B. Jenkins. *Left Behind: A Novel of the Earth's Last Days.* Wheaton, Illinois: Tyndale House Publishers, Inc., 1995.

_____. *Tribulation Force: The Continuing Drama of Those Left Behind.* Wheaton, Illinois: Tyndale House Publishers, Inc., 1996.

_____. *The Vanishings: Left Behind: The Kids.* Wheaton, Illinois: Tyndale House Publishers, Inc., 1998.

LaMott, Anne. *Plan B: Further Thoughts on Faith.* New York: Riverhead Books, 2005.

Levenson, Jon D. "Do Christians and Muslims worship the same God?" *The Christian Century,* April 20, 2004, pp. 32-33.

Long, Edward Leroy, Jr. *Peace Thinking in a Warring World: An Urgent Call for a New Approach to Peace.* Philadelphia: The Westminster Press, 1983.

Maalouf, Amin. *In the Name of Identity: Violence and the Need to Belong,* translated from the French by Barbara Bray. New York: Penguin Books, 2000.

Madsen, Ann N. *Making Their Own Peace: Twelve Women of Jerusalem.* New York: Lantern Books, 2003.

Mandela, Nelson, *Long Walk to Freedom: the Autobiography of Nelson Mandela,* abridged by Coco Cachalia and Marc Suttner. London, UK: Little, Brown and Co., Ltd., 1994.

McCarthy, Colman. *I'd Rather Teach Peace.* Maryknoll, New York: Orbis Books, 2003.

Merton, Thomas. *Passion for Peace: The Social Essays,* William H. Shannon, ed. New York: Crossroad, 1997.

Miller, Sara, "The Islamic Jesus," *The Christian Century,* January 2–9, 2002, pp. 20-24.

Mollenkott, Virginia Ramey, ed. *Women of Faith in Dialogue.* New York: Crossroad, 1990.

Moyers, Bill. *Speaking to Power, NOW with Bill Moyers Special Edition.* Broadcast December 26, 2003, on PBS. © Public Affairs Television. All rights reserved.

Murata, Sachiko and William C. Chittick. *The Vision of Islam.* St. Paul, Minnesota: Paragon House, 1994.

Musser, Donald W. and D. Dixon Sutherland, eds. *War Or Words? Interreligious Dialogue as an Instrument of Peace.* Cleveland: The Pilgrim Press, 2005.

Nasr, Seyyed Hossein. *The Heart of Islam.* HarperSanFrancisco, 2002.

National Conference of Catholic Bishops. "The Challenge of Peace: God's Promise and Our Response," The Pastoral Letter on War and Peace. United States Catholic Conference, Inc. 1983. (See Castelli, *The Bishops and the Bomb.*)

Nelson-Pallmeyer, Jack. *Is Religion Killing Us? Violence in the Bible and the Quran.* New York: Trinity Press International, 2003.

The New Oxford Annotated Bible: New Revised Standard Version, Michael D. Coogan, ed. New York: Oxford University Press, 2001.

O'Neill, Maura. *Women Speaking, Women Listening: Women in Interreligious Dialogue.* Maryknoll, New York: Orbis Books, 1990.

Patel, Eboo. "Editorial." *CrossCurrents,* Spring 2005, issue on "Current Issues in Interfaith Work," vol. 55, no. 1, pp. 4-7.

Peavy, Fran, U.S. ed. *I Remember/Sjeçam Se: Writings by Bosnian Women Refugees.* San Francisco: Aunt Lute Books, 1996.

Powers, Gerard F., Drew Christiansen, and Robert T. Hennemeyer, eds. *Peacemaking: Moral and Policy Challenges for a New World.* Washington, D.C.: United States Catholic Conference, Inc., 1994.

Queen Noor. *Leap of Faith: Memoirs of an Unexpected Life.* New York: Miramax Books, 2003.

Renard, John. *101 Questions and Answers on Islam.* New York: Gramercy Books, 1998.

Sacks, Jonathan. *The Dignity of Difference: How to Avoid the Clash of Civilizations.* New York: Continuum, 2003.

Sanneh, Lamin. "Do Christians and Muslims worship the same God?" *The Christian Century,* May 4, 2004, p. 35.

Schell, Jonathan. *The Unconquerable World: Power, Nonviolence, and the Will of the People.* New York: Henry Holt and Company, 2003.

Sharma, Arvind and Kathleen M. Dugan, eds. *A Dome of Many Colors: Religious Pluralism, Identity, and Unity.* Harrisburg, Pennsylvania: Trinity Press International, 1999.

Sherwin, Byron L. and Harold Kasimow, eds. John Paul II and Interreligious Dialogue. Maryknoll, New York: Orbis Books, 1999.

Smoch, David R., ed. *Interfaith Dialogue and Peacebuilding.* Washington, D.C.: United States Institute of Peace Press, 2002.

Speight, R. Marston. *Creating Interfaith Community.* New York: United Methodist Church General Board of Global Ministries, 2003.

Stanton, Elizabeth Cady. "The Worship of God in Man," in John Henry Barrows, *The World's Parliament of Religions, Volume II.* Chicago: The Parliament Publishing Company, 1893, pp. 1235-1236.

Stassen, Glen H. *Just Peacemaking: Transforming Initiatives for Justice and Peace.* Louisville, Kentucky: Westminster John Knox Press, 1992.

Suchocki, Marjorie. *Divinity and Diversity: A Christian Affirmation of Religious Pluralism.* Nashville: Abingdon Press, 2003.

Teasdale, Wayne and George Cairns, eds. *The Community of Religions, Voices, and Images of the Parliament of the World's Religions.* New York: Continuum, 1999.

Thangaraj, M. Thomas. *Relating to People of Other Religions: What Every Christian Needs to Know.* Nashville: Abingdon Press, 1997.

Titus, Murray T. *The Young Moslem Looks at Life.* New York: Friendship Press, 1937.

Trible, Phyllis and Letty M. Russell, eds. *Hagar, Sarah, and Their Children.* Louisville: Westminster John Knox Press, 2006.

Younan, Munib, *Witnessing for Peace: In Jerusalem and the World.* Minneapolis: Fortress Press, 2003.

Young, Ronald J. "A Case Study: American Christians, Jews, and Muslims Working Together for Middle East Peace," *Voices of the Religious Left: A Contemporary Sourcebook,* Rebecca T. Alpert, ed. Philadelphia: Temple University Press, 2000, pp. 265-272.

Volf, Miroslav. *Exclusion and Embrace: A Theological Exploration of Identity, Otherness and Reconciliation.* Nashville: Abingdon Press, 1996.

Waskow, Arthur. "We All Live in a Sukkah," *From the Ashes: A Spiritual Response to the Attack on America.* The editors of Beliefnet. Rodale, 2001, pp. 214-217.

Washington National Cathedral and the United States Institute of Peace. *Waging Peace: A Two-part Discussion of Religion-based Peacemaking.* Washington, DC: Washington National Cathedral, Program and Ministry.

Weatherhead, Leslie. *The Will of God.* New York: Abingdon-Cokesbury Press, 1944.

Whitney, Lawrence. "Beyond the Threefold Typology, Buddhist-Christian Monastic Dialogue." Unpublished paper, May 2004.

Woodberry, J. Dudley. "Do Christians and Muslims worship the same God?" *The Christian Century,* May 18, 2004, pp. 36-37.

Woodward, Kenneth L. "The Bible and the Qur'an, Searching the Holy Books for Roots of Conflict and Seeds of Reconciliation," *Newsweek,* February 11, 2002, pp. 51-57.

Wright, Christina. "The Interfaith Journey of an American Girl," *CrossCurrents,* Spring 2005, issue on "Current Issues in Interfaith Work," vol. 55, no. 1, pp. 121-129.

Yount, David. "Muslim-Christian Alliance Created." Scripps Howard News Service. *Finger Lakes Times,* July 1, 2004, p. 4A.

Zaleski, Carol. "Time Out for Allah," *The Christian Century,* June 15, 2004, p. 37.

STUDY GUIDE
FOR
SHALOM, SALAAM, PEACE

Pat Patterson

STUDY GUIDE CONTENTS

"One Earth, One Sky"

(Peace On Earth, Shanti, Salaam, Shalom)

Lyric by Alison Hubbard

Music by Kim Oler

One earth, one sky, one God on high, one peo - ple here be - low.

One bind-ing theme, one goal, one dream for all who live and grow:

Peace on earth, peace on earth, shan - ti, sa - laam, sha - lom,

peace on earth, peace on earth, shan - ti, sa - laam, sha - lom.

Each caring choice, each gentle voice can make the music ring.
Each mind and heart must do its part, each hand can help to bring
Peace on earth, peace on earth, shanti, salaam, shalom
peace on earth, peace on earth, shanti, salaam, shalom.

If all the shouts could turn to pray'rs amid the fiery rush
the whole world 'round would hear the sound, an unfamiliar hush:
Peace on earth, peace on earth, shanti, salaam, shalom,
peace on earth, peace on earth, shanti, salaam, shalom.

Available in various choral voicings from the music publisher:
Helium Music / 12 Brighton Place / Huntington, NY 11743
KimOler@Gmail.com

INTRODUCTION

This mission study has a dual focus: furthering interfaith understanding and cooperation, and peacemaking. What hinders? What helps? The hope is that people of all faiths will work together to build peace.

This study guide accompanies the study book *Shalom, Salaam, Peace.* It is designed to assist those guiding the study, primarily in United Methodist Women's Schools of Christian Mission. It can also serve local churches and other study settings—denominational, ecumenical, or interfaith. It is important to recognize that while the study includes diverse voices, it is written primarily from Christian perspectives. Interfaith groups, therefore, will need to arrange ways to balance other religious points of view.

The guide attempts to help prepare persons for leadership by offering ways of thinking about the purpose and significance of the study, as well as sensitivities of heart and mind. It also suggests how to get ready to be a study leader, to set up the space, and to find resources. Concretely, too, this guide provides outlines or lesson plans for four two-hour sessions. Getting ready for the study requires first and foremost a careful reading of the study text. It is also valuable for the study leader and potential study participants to begin collecting related materials from newspapers, magazines, Web sites, and personal experience in order to enrich the study and make it currently relevant.

The study aims to engage us in looking at how Jews, Muslims, and Christians, from the three Abrahamic religions, understand God and value peace. Using our experience as Christian people, but also referring to the thoughts of others, it leads us into looking seriously at those views and realities that are obstacles to peace. It moves us toward examining keys to achieving a world culture of peace. Furthermore, it introduces us to women who are involved in peacemaking and invites us to cultivate peace in our own hearts as well as in our communities and world.

As we look around our home areas and the wider world, we see places where tensions are great and misunderstandings rife between people of different religions. We cannot but think of Israel and Palestine and of the U.S., Iraq, and other countries in the Middle East, as well as Afghanistan and South Asia. And we cannot ignore incidents of hate crimes in our own country. We recognize that just beneath the surface—for history is a very lively reality—are the points where the crimes of the Crusades and the Holocaust suddenly appear like giant icebergs blocking smooth passage. And the ghosts of their victims rise up to challenge genuine bridge building and peace building in our time.

SIGNIFICANCE OF THE STUDY

Peace in Our Time Is Critical.

Despite hopes that the end of the Cold War would bring us peace and peace dividends for our economy, our nation has continued to gear up for war. And the world has become a more dangerous place. Local and regional conflicts have continued to occur in various parts of the world. Many of these are based on ethnic, religious, economic, and political differences. Since 9/11, terrorism has been identified as the primary reason for preventive war and perpetual war. Increasingly, the peaking of oil and natural gas production warns us that resource wars are also on the scene. Getting at the root causes of discontent, scarcity, conflict, and terrorism, however, has been secondary to military response. We need urgently to address the world's grievances as well as its aspirations.

Building Justice and Peace Will Take the Efforts of All,
Especially People of Faith.

Religious people share many common values needed to design strategies to prevent and resolve conflict, as well as to build peace. The media report more and more religious tensions. The conflict in Northern Ireland between Catholics and Protestants is one long-time tragedy. We hear, too, of violence between Hindus and Muslims, Buddhists and Hindus, Jews and Muslims, and Christians and Muslims. Yet it is often too easy to oversimplify and blame religious differences, when political, economic, and cultural factors must also be carefully examined. From all sides, we must urgently work together.

Diversity in Religion and Culture Is a Reality in Our World.

It is essential for peace that we know about each other and relate in respectful ways. In our global village we hear about each other, but often the news is distorted or partial. We don't have sufficient opportunities to meet and debate. Our governments too often focus on narrow self-interest—economic, political, military. They neglect programs that insure the well-being of all, promote understanding, and devise ways to share decisions and responsibility for justice and peace.

In the Last Four Decades, Our Nation's Diversity Has Increased.

Earlier immigrations from Europe involved Protestant, Catholic, and Jewish differences and took years to work through, even though sharing a common tradition in the Bible. In recent years U.S. cultural and religious diversity has grown more broadly, particularly with the addition of people from Asia and the Middle East. Our history of racism requires us to be especially vigilant so that newer ethnic and religious groups do not suffer the discriminatory policies and often violent treatment given first to Native Americans and subsequently to African Americans, Mexicans, Japanese Americans, and others. Religious intolerance often fosters conflict.

Building Peace at Home and Abroad Challenges Religious People to Engage in Self-Examination, Active Dialogue, and Cooperation.

As Christians who have been in the majority in the U.S. and dominant in the powerful Western world, we need to confront our sense of superiority and power. We have a special opportunity to deepen our faith and Christian discipleship and to enrich our spirituality in cooperation with people of other faiths. We need to look squarely at what helps and what hinders us in developing a truly peaceful, just, and pluralistic society and world community. If we are to have peace, we must learn to respect and be friends with all.

SENSITIVITIES: HEART-SETS AND MIND-SETS

Discussing Our Faith and Being Open to People of Other Faiths Is a Sensitive Matter.

Many of us have a history of believing that Christianity is the only true religion. We have had little experience with people of other faiths and the ways that they express their reverence for God and their spiritual gifts. In a time of so much change and fear, we are often defensive about what we cherish, especially our religion. We often see the religious doctrines and practices of others as alien and incomplete, and sometimes even heathen or idolatrous. We have been taught that there is no way to God except through Jesus Christ. We have taken absolute statements about Christianity, and our own brand of theology, as the final word on religious truth.

Even Christian Diversity Is a Major Challenge for Us.

We sometimes disagree among ourselves as to what is really Christian, who Jesus truly is, and what he taught. So we find that taking the step to respectful dialogue with people of other faiths is almost more than we can manage. Meanwhile the world cries for peace, tolerance, and harmony. As we come face to face with God in Christ over and over again, we are struck by the love, acceptance, and inclusion of the Master and the first-century church seeking to walk in his footsteps. Jesus' encounter with the woman at the well

154

(John 4:1-42)—woman, Samaritan, religiously different—reminds us of his remarkable openness. We remember, too, Philip's meeting with the Ethiopian eunuch and Peter's dream of radical inclusion, with the great sheet full of creatures and the voice saying, "What God has made clean, you must not call profane" (Acts 10:15). We recall the vision of the Roman centurion Cornelius (Acts 10:1-6) that led him to a Peter who was now open to the questions of his soul. The work of the Holy Spirit surely is God's embrace of the whole varied world of God's daughters and sons. Perhaps struggles for inclusiveness in the church can be a model and foretaste for inclusiveness within the world and among faith communities.

Can We Commit Ourselves to a Mind-Set and Heart-Set That Will Open Us to Interfaith Dialogue, Peacemaking, and Cooperation?

Can we relax in our faith, drop our defensiveness, be open to learning from and about others, and try to imagine a God's-eye-view of the world? A view that weeps over all the victims of the South Asia tsunami and the war with Iraq and attends to the spiritual as well as physical needs of all broken, grieving people who pray in many ways? A view that respects the chanting of Buddhists, the call to worship of Muslims, the prayers of Christians, the lamps and chants of Hindus, the Shabbat services of Jews, as people pray for healing, renewal, and peace?

In this study then, can we

1. Focus on peace with justice and other concerns essential to survival and fullness of life for the whole human family?
2. Draw on spiritual and religious resources that can lead us to affirm diversity and pluralism and build a peaceful world?
3. Respect the spiritual and religious traditions and paths taken by a variety of peoples and cultures in their search for ultimate meaning?
4. Be open to learning more about other religions and to positioning ourselves for new conversation and cooperation?

5. Deal with our assumptions about Christianity by deepening our relationship with God and increasing our awareness of other spiritualities?

6. Analyze the ways racism, bigotry, prejudice, and national superiority have shaped us and our culture, often cutting us off from richer community?

7. Confront our addiction to violence and war as the solution to conflict and do genuine peace building in pluralistic community?

Essential to our life together in the study group will be prayer, open and patient dialogue, searching minds and compassionate hearts, and profound commitment to peace.

PREPARING TO LEAD

1. As a study leader, the first step is to read the study book *Shalom, Salaam, Peace*. Read it through once, and then begin to go through it section by section with the appropriate parts of the study guide. Jot down ideas and questions as they occur to you. This overall view of the study will give you confidence as you proceed.

2. Review the bibliography, and choose some books that will enrich your understanding and enable the study. Glance at them before buying or borrowing them, looking for the most relevant content and judging them for readability. Read these in relation to the sections of the book in which these subjects are treated.

3. Scan Web sites that also help broaden your knowledge and comprehension. Make notes, so you can make recommendations to class participants regarding what is most useful. Print out what may be of the greatest help to the study.

4. Clip articles and pictures from newspapers and magazines that can be used for bulletin boards or special assignments, especially about conflict situations where religious tensions play a role.

5. Collect materials and prepare files as resources for the two groups in the final session as assigned at the end of Session I. One is the annotated list of organizations that work for peace, and another is materials and involvements of United Methodist Women and of The United Methodist Church.

6. Locate posters that show scenes from Muslim, Jewish, and Christian religious life and sites. Also look for posters that show and/or oppose conflict and promote peace, especially among people of different faiths.

7. Identify and visit a mosque, a synagogue, or temple in your community. Find out what kind of peacemaking these folks are involved in. See if this house of worship might be open to visits from groups who are doing the study. Or, ask if religious leaders or laypersons might be willing to come to a meeting of your study group and speak about the relationship between their faith and their commitment to working for peace.

8. At some point of readiness, begin to develop your own class outlines by going systematically through the study book and the guide. Even as you develop your course outline, remain flexible and note options that may become clear to you after you begin to interact with the group members.

9. Cultivate an attitude and practice of prayer that will express the spiritual foundations of the study, undergird the aims of the study by building interreligious respect and peacemaking, and enable caring community and discussion among the participants.

SETTING UP THE STUDY SPACE

1. Position chairs in the meeting room in a circle or semicircle, arranged to help everyone feel comfortable and included. Allow for small group discussion, imagining how small groups of three or four can easily arrange themselves, and how larger groups of

six to nine may be placed within the space available. Investigate the availability of adjoining rooms or the hallway for small groups. Especially for the larger groups, consider issues of hearing and visibility.

2. Arrange for newsprint and markers for use during the study. If there is a chalkboard available, be sure you have the appropriate writing instruments and erasers.

3. Decorate the room with materials that relate especially to Section I of the study book. If possible, have some parts of the display remain throughout the study. Have others that change from one section and session of the study to the next. Try to make the room both attractive and informative.

4. Have a resource table with books, magazines, and other materials for browsing. This may also include printouts from Web sites that are especially helpful and accessible.

5. Be sure to have enough hymnbooks or songbooks for the participants. You may also want to introduce new songs by having copies made for distribution.

6. Plan to have Bibles or printed sheets with the daily Bible passages and discussion questions to hand out.

7. If you anticipate using audiotapes, videos, or DVDs, be sure to reserve the needed equipment, including a screen.

8. If you need help in keeping track of resources, setting up new displays, keeping the space in order, and rearranging the chairs, ask for a small group of volunteers to help you with these housekeeping chores.

IDENTIFYING RESOURCES

1. Recognize that this study is an ongoing project. Review the previous study on "Creating Interfaith Community" and see what linkages can be made. Because resources are numerous, urge

the group members to see the possibilities for continuing education sessions in their communities, drawing on interfaith materials and skills in peacemaking.

2. Carefully read the study book *Shalom, Salaam, Peace,* and note places where resources are mentioned, especially the bibliography at the end and the list of groups and Web sites in Section IV.

3. Look for the special mission study issues of *Response* and *New World Outlook,* as well as articles in past issues that deal with themes related to this study. *Fellowship,* the magazine of the Fellowship of Reconciliation (FOR), is another good source.

4. Study newspapers and magazines for articles regarding interfaith dialogue, places of conflict, and promising peace possibilities.

5. Visit synagogues and mosques in your area. Ask if someone might be available to talk with the group about her or his faith and peacemaking. See what kind of projects this house of worship is engaged in regarding peace and interfaith dialogue.

6. Look at the United Methodist Women's Reading List and note the books, both fiction and nonfiction, that have some relationship with the study.

7. Make a list of professors and courses in your local college or university that deal with other religions, interfaith relations, and peacemaking.

8. Find Web sites that give you more information about Muslims, Jews, and other topics of interest.

9. Explore the availability of videos and DVDs. Preview those that seem most useful and evaluate them for the study series or for later continuing education and follow-up in your community. Public television catalogs may be helpful to you. One series, "A Force More Powerful," is about nonviolence in a number of world situations. The Pluralism Project at Harvard may be another source: http://www.pluralism.org/affiliates/antell/

PEACE AND THE ABRAHAMIC RELIGIONS

A. STATING OUR GOALS

In this introductory session, using Section I of the study book *Shalom, Salaam, Peace*, we aim to

- Establish community within which to explore interfaith peacemaking;
- Look at examples of openness to people of other faiths;
- Examine key commonalities and differences among the three Abrahamic faiths;
- Identify and pray for conflict situations made tense by religious and other differences.

B. INTRODUCTION AND BRIEF WORSHIP (10 minutes)

Introduce the study, using some key points from the Introduction, Significance of the Study, and Sensitivities. Encourage openness, dialogue, and soul-searching prayer.

Sing "This Is My Song, O God of All the Nations," *The United Methodist Hymnal*, no. 437.

Have a prayer for peace, interfaith understanding, and the life of this study group.

C. BIBLE STUDY (25 minutes)
JESUS AND THE SAMARITANS: INTERFAITH ENCOUNTER

1. Read Aloud This Background Material to Set Up the Discussion

Jesus' relationship with the Samaritans is a window into how we may relate to people of other faiths. Think of the story of the

Samaritan woman at the well, the parable of the good Samaritan, and the ten lepers of whom one is Samaritan, to understand who the Samaritans were in Jesus' time.

Living in central Palestine, with Galilee to the north and Judea to the south, the Samaritans were descendants of Israelites from the Northern Kingdom. The break between them and other Jews had taken place centuries before, in 721 B.C.E., and was recounted in 2 Kings 17. Conquered by the Assyrians, some Israelites were taken away into exile for many years. Meanwhile, foreign colonists were brought into the land. While not seen as Gentiles, the Samaritans were considered ritually impure due to intermarriage and their mixed and different religious beliefs. The worship of the Samaritans was centered on their holy mountain of Gerizim, not the Temple at Jerusalem. They focused only on the Pentateuch, the first five books of Scripture. They were scorned and discriminated against. Usually Jewish travelers avoided passing through Samaria by taking a route east of the Jordan River.

Jesus saw his ministry both within his own Jewish people and outward to the Gentiles. His openness to all people regardless of religion, sex, nationality, ethnicity, class, and party was remarkable and radical. From the beginning he spoke of how God worked among foreigners and people of other faiths. In Luke 4:22-30, while speaking at the synagogue in Nazareth, Jesus recalled that in Elijah's time, a time of hunger and drought, among all the poor widows, it was the widow at Sidon to whom Elijah came and promised that "the jar of meal will not be emptied and the jug of oil will not fail until the day that the Lord sends rain on the earth" (1 Kings 17:14). And again he said that among the many lepers in Israel in Elisha's time, it was Naaman the Syrian, who was healed through the prophet's power (2 Kings 5:1-14).

2. Study of the Bible Passages on Samaritans and Jesus

Ask everyone quietly to review the story of the woman at the well in John 4:3-30, thinking of what this encounter says to us today in

interfaith dialogue. Provide Bibles or copies of the passage mentioned. If participants have the study book, ask them to turn to the
questions below, or make a copy for each person.

After five to seven minutes of personal study, hold a quick but
open discussion of the following questions:

a. Why do you think Jesus had to go through Samaria?

b. What brought Jesus and the woman together? What did they
offer each other?

c. When the woman tried to start an argument about the right
place to worship, how did Jesus instead shift to common
ground?

d. In what ways is it significant that she is one of the first persons to whom Jesus reveals that he is the Messiah, the Christ?

e. What did the woman do about her meeting and discussion
with Jesus? How is this crossing of boundaries made possible?

f. What do two other Gospel stories about Samaritans tell us
about Jesus and his ministry in relationship to these outsider
people?
—the parable of the good Samaritan, Luke 10:27-37
—the story of the ten lepers, Luke 17:11-19

3. In Conclusion and Review

In what ways do Jesus' encounters with Samaritans relate to the following and give us some sense of direction in our interfaith relations?

- intentionality about meeting people
- consciousness of exclusion and discrimination
- appreciation for others and their gifts
- openness to dialogue
- establishing common ground
- mutuality in giving and receiving

D. GETTING ACQUAINTED AND SHARING EXPERIENCES
(20 minutes)

Give each group member a small questionnaire using the three questions below:

1. Briefly give your name and where you come from. Describe one experience of involvement in peacemaking and how it affected you.
2. Describe one experience of relating to Jewish or Muslim persons, including how you felt and what you learned.
3. Have you been involved in peacemaking or community action with people of other faiths? Briefly describe.

For five minutes have people quickly jot down their replies in simple outline form. Now form small groups of three or four persons who do not know each other well. Have the participants introduce themselves, asking each person to share her or his response to question 1, going around the circle until all have shared responses to each question.

Invite a few people to list the types of experiences mentioned in their get-acquainted groups. Later in the study there may be an opportunity to share more about these experiences. Collect the forms for the study leaders to use as background information about the participants.

E. UNDERSTANDING THE THREE ABRAHAMIC RELIGIONS
(55 minutes)

Section I of the study book deals with Judaism, Islam, and Christianity, their commonalities and their uniqueness. If Jewish and Muslim speakers are available, invite them for this section. Good films may also provide important understanding. Otherwise a group process is offered below.

1. Listing Similarities

For about ten minutes, referring especially to the Introduction of the text, ask group members to identify points of similarity among the three religious traditions and to discuss what these mean. As each point is mentioned, write it on newsprint or a chalkboard. These may include

    a. All come from the Abrahamic tradition.

    b. All three are monotheistic, that is, believe in one God.

    c. All are people of the Book.

    d. All hold Jerusalem to be the Holy City.

2. Looking at the Three Unique Traditions

Form three small groups. Each group will analyze one of the three religions. Refer to the Section I introduction on "Peace and the Abrahamic Religions," as well as

    Chapter 1 on "Shalom, the Lord and the Tanakh"—Judaism

    Chapter 2 on "Salaam, Allah, and the Holy Qur'an"—Islam

    Chapter 3 on "The Peace of Christ, the Triune God, and the New Testament"—Christianity.

Give each group a newsprint page to use in making notes on the religion assigned. Allow approximately fifteen minutes to discuss and describe the following:

    a. Name and understanding of God, including believers' relationship with God;

    b. Meaning and importance of peace;

    c. Points to clarify or continue to study.

3. Trying a Trialogue in Pursuit of Peace

In the next exercise, bring two people from each of the three groups into pluralistic groups of six. Have the participants pretend to be followers of the religion they have been studying. Invite them to enter into dialogue with each other for about twenty minutes.

The following questions may help stimulate the discussion:

    a. How do we understand and worship God? Differences. Similarities.

    b. How do we view Jesus?

c. What place does peace play in our religions? Differences. Similarities.

d. What in our histories has led us to trust or distrust one another?

e. What are some historical situations today where working together for peace is essential?

4. Sharing the Trialogue and Identifying Places of Conflict

Draw the entire group back together. Talk about how they felt in this trialogue situation.

a. Were there any new insights or major questions?

b. What are challenges for Jewish, Muslim, and Christian people in working for peace? What past history makes the task of cooperative peacemaking difficult?

c. What are places in the world today where religion is an ingredient in conflict, especially confrontations among Jews, Muslims, and Christians?

d. How can we be more aware of places of tension and war and the possibilities for our churches to join in contributing to peace?

F. CLOSING WITH INTERCESSORY PRAYER

Pray in silence for people in the conflicts mentioned. Have the conflict places listed on newsprint or chalkboard. Sing together "Dona Nobis Pacem," *The United Methodist Hymnal,* no. 376.

G. ANNOUNCING ASSIGNMENTS

Allow five minutes or so at the end of the session. Copy the following list of assignments and distribute. Have people indicate their willingness to take on one of the four tasks for Session IV. List their names on the board.

FOR THE NEXT SESSION

1. Read study book Section II and its four chapters on "Obstacles

to Breaking Cycles of Violence." For each of the four chapters, ask yourself these questions and make notes:

- Define the problem. What exactly is this obstacle or hindrance to ending violence and working with people of other faiths to build peace?
- What are the underlying assumptions behind this? How do we judge their truth?
- How do these obstacles play out in our society and influence us? Give examples.
- Who benefits from these positions that undergird violence? Who is harmed?
- What can we do to overcome or transform these obstacles and build foundations for peace?

2. For the Bible study next time, ask eight people to be prepared for the dramatic reading of Acts 10:1-36. Ask someone to coordinate, to assign the following parts, and to direct. The parts of Peter and Cornelius should be assigned to the same persons in all four scenes.

Verses 1-8, narrator in Cornelius's story, the angel, Cornelius;
Verses 9-16, narrator in Peter's story, the voice, and Peter;
Verses 17-23, narrator in Peter's story, Peter, the Spirit, and Cornelius' two messengers;
Verses 24-36, new narrator, Peter, and Cornelius.

PLANNING AHEAD FOR THE FOURTH AND FINAL SESSION

1. For everyone: Write and be prepared to share your autobiography of concern about peace and involvement in peacemaking. Include your growing consciousness, people who influenced you, relationship to your faith, places where you found opposition and support, and points of connection with people of other faiths.

Or, consider another person (a relative, friend, someone you admire), and write a biography of that person's peacemaking, using the same kinds of elements.

2. **For a committee of two or three:** Make an annotated list of organizations that work for peace. Include groups that witness to diversity, human rights, equality, reconciliation, interfaith dialogue and cooperation. List address, phone, and Web site if available. Prepare the list in print to share with the whole group. (The leader should prepare a file in advance to introduce some groups and help the committee get started in its work.)

3. **For a committee of two or three:** Study United Methodist Women and United Methodist Church materials, and identify points of involvement in peacemaking and support for key values that support peace. Look at such sources as *Response* magazine, *Call to Prayer and Self-Denial*, United Methodist Church *Book of Resolutions, New World Outlook*, the Advance catalog, the United Methodist Women's Reading List, General Board of Global Ministries and Board of Church and Society programs. (The leader should prepare a collection of resources to assist the committee in doing its work.)

4. **For a committee of two:** Devise a "We Will Be Together" litany regarding violent situations in the U.S. and in the world today and ways to join in peacemaking. Use Mary Farrell Bednarowski's narrative in Chapter 11 as a model. You may even quote some of her phrases as you frame your litany.

5. **For a committee of two:** Plan a closing worship of fifteen minutes for the end of the study. Bring together "Let Peace Begin with Me" and the conflict and peace possibilities of the wider world. Consider songs, time of meditation, prayer, act of commitment. One option for singing is "In the Midst of New Dimensions" from *The Faith We Sing,* #2238. Join with the litany group above to include its work in the worship.

OBSTACLES TO BREAKING CYCLES OF VIOLENCE

A. STATING OUR GOALS

- Explore different positions that people hold regarding other faiths and the openness that enables interfaith relations and peacemaking.
- Examine obstacles to peace, such as, a religion's exclusive truth claims, violence ascribed to God in Scriptures and culture, state-sponsored violence, and our addiction to war and violence.
- Evaluate these obstacles in light of the identity and message of Jesus and the Christian community, as well as alternative models of peacemaking.

B. BRIEF WORSHIP (5 minutes)

Sing "One Earth, One Sky" (p. 150) or "Many Gifts, One Spirit" (*The United Methodist Hymnal*, no. 114) and pray for unity among all kinds of people.

C. BIBLE STUDY (25 minutes)
PETER AND CORNELIUS: REACHING OUT

Read Acts 10:1-36: Have people do this story as a dramatic reading. Divide the parts as follows and have people standing in their places ready to read. With movement, as well as the words, interpret what is happening in the story.

Scene I, verses 1-8—On one side of the stage have the narrator in Cornelius's story, the angel, and Cornelius.
Scene II, verses 9-16—On the other side have the narrator in Peter's story, the voice, and Peter.

Scene III, verses 17-23—In the center have the two messengers and Peter come together, with Peter's narrator and the Spirit on Peter's side of the stage.

Scene IV, verses 24-36—In the encounter between Cornelius and Peter have a new narrator but the same Peter and Cornelius.

In the whole group, discuss reactions to this passage.

- What was the problem for Cornelius, his obstacle? What does the vision of Cornelius tell him and us?
- What was the obstacle in Peter's understanding? What does the vision of Peter say, and how does Peter change as a result of it?
- What meaning does this story have for us as we discuss interfaith dialogue and relations?

D. BEING RELIGIOUS IN A RELIGIOUSLY DIVERSE WORLD
(35 minutes)

1. DISCUSSION ROUND I. For fifteen minutes in small groups of three or four persons, read each of the following quotations and then consider the quotation in light of the questions that follow them:

a. "We All Live in a Sukkah," Rabbi Arthur Waskow: "There are only wispy walls and leaky roofs between us. The planet is in fact one interwoven web of life. The command to love my neighbor as I do myself is not an admonition to be nice: It is a statement of truth like the law of gravity. For my neighbor and myself are interwoven." And Rabbi Waskow prays: "Spread over all of us your sukkah of shalom." (p. 13)

b. Himmatilla's letter to Allison: "We have to put aside religious differences, race differences, class differences, and any other differences which put us apart from each other. We shouldn't be ignorant about each other. This increases the gap between people and they start guessing about each other, which obviously leads to misguidance. We have so many Ones: One planet, One future, One nature, One origin, One heart." (p. 16)

   c. David Benke's prayer at Yankee Stadium: "The strength we have is the power of love. And the power of love you have received from God, for God is love. So take the hand of the one next to you now and join me in prayer on this field of dreams turned into God's house of prayer." (p. 35)

1. What are our reactions to the statements and images of these spokespersons featured in the study book? Who are they? Listen to their words and consider their images.

2. How do we balance our own faith commitment and loyalty with the desire to be tolerant and open?

3. What do these affirmations mean for our life and faith?

2. DISCUSSION ROUND II. For ten minutes, talk about the following:

- Why was David Benke's prayer so controversial? What different perspectives are operating in his case?

- How do you feel about participating in an interfaith event?

- Are you helped to understand the controversy, as well as to clarify your own choices, as you recognize in the list that follows, the ways that different people describe their relations with other religions?

  - Some people consider themselves exclusivist, believing that their religion alone is true.

  - Some are inclusivist, feeling that their religion is superior, although others may have part of the truth, but not the full truth that their own religion has.

  - Still others are pluralist, holding that God is one and that people experience and believe in God differently from a variety of cultures, traditions, and perspectives.

3. DISCUSSION ROUND III. Now consider this story and its haunting question:

"In Chaim Potok's novel *The Book of Lights*, a young rabbi from Brooklyn, on leave from his post in Korea during the Korean War, travels for the first time to Japan. One afternoon he stands with a

Jewish friend before what is perhaps a Shinto shrine with a clear mirror in the sanctum or perhaps a Buddhist shrine with an image of the Bodhisattva of Compassion.... The altar is lit by the soft light of a tall lamp. Sunlight streams in the door. The two young men observe with fascination a man standing before the altar, his hands pressed together before him, his eyes closed. He is rocking slightly. He is clearly engaged in what we would call prayer. The rabbi turns to his companion and says:

"'Do you think our God is listening to him, John?'

"'I don't know, chappy. I never thought of it.'

"'Neither did I until now. If He's not listening, why not? If He is listening, then—well, what are we all about, John?'"

(From Diana Eck's *Encountering God: A Spiritual Journey from Bozeman to Banaras*, Boston: Beacon Press, 1993; p. 166.)

For ten minutes, discuss:

a. Does our God hear the prayers of people of other faiths? Think about Muslims in Iraq and Afghanistan in the midst of war. Think of people in Palestine and Israel. Think of people in south Asia overwhelmed by the tsunami. Does our God hear the prayers of people of other faiths?

b. Is there perhaps a problem even in using the phrase "our" God? Whose God is God?

MEDITATION AND PRAYER

Spend a few moments in silence and meditation. A possible prayer might be this:

O God, you are wider and deeper than I can ever comprehend. You have created all people with hunger for you in their hearts. People respond in so many different ways. I come to you uniquely from my own life, culture, and religious tradition. Help me grow in my understanding. Help me honor the way others come to you. In Jesus Christ, I pray. Amen

E. WORKING GROUPS ON VIOLENCE (45 minutes)

Form three working groups. Spend thirty minutes in discussion of a chapter (assign one chapter to each group) and the five guiding questions.

Then for ten to fifteen minutes, plan ways to express your conclusions, main ideas, or questions through drama, panel discussion, or other forms. Be ready in the next class period to do a ten-minute presentation, including both creative expression and summary of main points (spoken or written).

1. Violence of God in Sacred Texts and Popular Culture—Chapter 5
2. State-Sponsored Violence—Chapter 6
3. Human Violence as Giver of Meaning—Chapter 7

QUESTIONS TO GUIDE THE WORKING GROUPS

1. Define the problem. What exactly is this obstacle or hindrance to ending violence and working with people of other faiths to build peace?
2. What are the underlying assumptions? How do we judge their truth?
3. How does this obstacle play out in our society and influence us? Give examples.
4. Who benefits from these positions that undergird violence? Who is harmed?
5. What can we do to overcome or transform these obstacles and build foundations for peace?

F. ANNOUNCING ASSIGNMENTS

1. Read Section III on "Keys to Achieving a World Culture of Peace." Be sure to read all four chapters.
2. Refine and be prepared to make your presentations about "Obstacles to Peace," using no more than ten minutes per group.
3. Continue working on special tasks for the fourth and last session.

KEYS TO ACHIEVING
A WORLD CULTURE OF PEACE

A. STATING OUR GOALS

1. Continue to look at obstacles to peace.
2. Explore the biblical, spiritual, and social power of nonviolence in dealing with conflict.
3. Examine keys to peace such as embracing diversity, working for equality and justice, practicing forgiveness and reconciliation, and engaging in interfaith dialogue and cooperation.
4. Find ways to support values that undergird peace and interfaith dialogue.

B. BRIEF WORSHIP (10 minutes)

Sing "Hymn for Peacemaking" at the beginning of Chapter 10, to the tune of "Come, Thou Long-Expected Jesus," (*The United Methodist Hymnal*, no. 196). Have a prayer, with each person contributing one sentence while thinking of the earth from outer space, thinking of the whole world as God might see it.

C. BIBLE STUDY (45 minutes)
JESUS' ARREST AND ENCOUNTER WITH VIOLENCE

1. Discuss the Content
   a. What is the context in which Jesus lived and carried on his ministry? For example, read Luke 13:1-3. This passage refers to an uprising against Pontius Pilate in the year 26 after he had confiscated Temple funds to build a huge aqueduct. He pretended to meet the protesters but then gave the signal to

the occupation army to club them to death. What might repentance mean in this context? (A useful book is *Jesus and Empire* by Richard A. Horsley. Minneapolis: Fortress Press, 2003.)

b. How did Jesus navigate the dangerous waters of Roman imperial occupation, the collaboration of Jewish political and religious authorities, and the anger of insurgents?

c. How did Jesus' presentation of the kingdom of God (or God's reign) offer a counterforce or alternative to the oppression of the Roman Empire?

2. Read the Four Gospel Accounts of Jesus' Arrest

Ask for four persons to read the passages aloud. Note discussion points on newsprint or chalkboard. After each account, briefly discuss these questions:

a. How does Jesus deal with his arrest?

b. What appears to be the reason that he does not resist?

c. Does the fact that he does not resist mean that he is passive?

Mark 14:46-49: "Then they laid hands on him and arrested him. But one of those who stood near drew his sword and struck the slave of the high priest, cutting off his ear. Then Jesus said to them, 'Have you come out with swords and clubs to arrest me as though I were a bandit? Day after day I was with you in the temple teaching, and you did not arrest me. But let the scriptures be fulfilled.' "

Luke 22:49-53: "When those who were around him saw what was coming, they asked, 'Lord, should we strike with the sword?' Then one of them struck the slave of the high priest and cut off his right ear. But Jesus said, 'No more of this!' And he touched his ear and healed him. Then Jesus said to the chief priests, the officers of the temple police, and the elders who had come for him, 'Have you come out with swords and clubs as if I were a bandit? When I was with you day after day in the temple, you did not lay hands on me. But this is your hour, and the power of darkness!' "

John 18:3-12: "So Judas brought a detachment of soldiers together with police from the chief priests and the Pharisees, and they came there with lanterns and torches and weapons. Then Jesus, knowing all that was to happen to him, came forward and asked them, 'Whom are you looking for?' They answered, 'Jesus of Nazareth.' Jesus replied, 'I am he.' Judas, who betrayed him, was standing with them. When Jesus said to them, 'I am he,' they stepped back and fell to the ground. Again he asked them, 'Whom are you looking for?' And they said, 'Jesus of Nazareth.' Jesus answered, 'I told you that I am he. So if you are looking for me, let these men go.' This was to fulfill the word that he had spoken, 'I did not lose a single one of those whom you gave me.' Then Simon Peter, who had a sword, drew it, struck the high priest's slave, and cut off his right ear. The slave's name was Malchus. Jesus said to Peter, 'Put your sword back into its sheath. Am I not to drink the cup that the Father has given me?' So the soldiers, their officer, and the Jewish police arrested Jesus and bound him."

Matthew 26:48-56: "Now the betrayer had given them a sign, saying, 'The one I will kiss is the man; arrest him.' At once he came up to Jesus and said, 'Greetings, Rabbi!' and kissed him. Jesus said to him, 'Friend, do what you are here to do.' Then they came and laid hands on Jesus and arrested him. Suddenly, one of those with Jesus put his hand on his sword, drew it, and struck the slave of the high priest, cutting off his ear. Then Jesus said to him, 'Put your sword back into its place; for all who take the sword will perish by the sword. Do you think that I cannot appeal to my Father, and he will at once send me more than twelve legions of angels? But how then would the scriptures be fulfilled, which say it must happen in this way?' At that hour Jesus said to the crowds, 'Have you come out with swords and clubs to arrest me as though I were a bandit? Day after day I sat in the temple teaching, and you did not arrest me. But all this has taken place, so that the scriptures of the prophets may be fulfilled.' "

3. Reflect on Where Jesus Stood on Violence

    a. What light do the four Gospels shed on how Jesus dealt with violence against him as he was being arrested? What appear to be the various reasons why Jesus did not resist arrest or allow his disciples to fight for him?

b. Do you think that Jesus had a choice as to whether he would end up dying in Jerusalem? How do you deal with the seeming contradiction between the idea that he was fated to die and that he died because of his faithfulness?

c. What do you think is Jesus' message to his followers then and to us now about nonviolence and peacemaking? How does his life inform us in our work of peacemaking in the face of confrontation and violence?

Be sure that the following explanations for Jesus' nonviolence are included in the discussion. Consider whether they are likely to be Jesus' reasons, interpretations of those around him, or later additions to the story. Also think of how the idea of the three wills of God (below) might give us helpful ways of thinking about Jesus' life and death.

- Prophecies that the Messiah must die
- This is the hour when darkness will prevail
- Commonsense fact that before such force his disciples could not prevail
- Concern for the safety of his disciples
- Sense that his mission from God leads him to this end
- The use of violence breeds violence
- The entire witness of Jesus is nonviolent and redemptive

D. THE WILL OF GOD

In the midst of World War II, Leslie Weatherhead, in his useful little book *The Will of God* (New York and Nashville: Abingdon-Cokesbury Press, 1944), identified three ways of looking at the will of God, both in the death of Jesus and in our lives. He speaks of

1. The intentional will of God
2. The circumstantial will of God
3. The ultimate will of God

Consider his views of God's will and the cross as Weatherhead (pp. 12–13) elaborates:

"1. Was it God's intention from the beginning that Jesus should go to the Cross? I think the answer to that question must be No. I don't think Jesus thought that at the beginning of his ministry. He came with the *intention* that men should follow him, not kill him. The discipleship of men, not the death of Christ, was the intentional will of God, or, if you like, God's ideal purpose—and I sometimes wish that in common language we could keep the phrase 'the will of God' for the intentional will of God."

"2. But when circumstances wrought by men's evil set up such a dilemma that Christ was compelled either to die or to run away, then *in those circumstances* the Cross was the will of God, but only in those circumstances which were themselves the fruit of evil. In those circumstances any other way was unworthy and impossible, and it was in this sense that our Lord said, 'Nevertheless not what I will, but what thou wilt.' "

"3. Then there is the third sense in which we use the phrase 'the will of God,' when we mean God's ultimate goal, the purposefulness of God—which, in spite of evil and, as we shall see, even through evil, arrives, with nothing of value lost, at the same goal as would have been reached if the intentional will of God could have been carried through without frustration.... So, in regard to the Cross, God achieved his final goal not simply in spite of the Cross but through it. He achieved a great redemption and realized his ultimate will in as full a sense as he would have done if his intentional will had not been temporarily defeated."

E. PRESENTATIONS FROM PREVIOUS SESSION BY THREE GROUPS (40 minutes)

1. Violence of God in Sacred Texts and Popular Christian Culture
2. State-Sponsored Violence
3. Human Violence as Giver of Meaning

In the entire group, provide some time for response to the presentations one by one, including experiences, other ideas or solutions, and ongoing questions. Refer back to Guiding Questions as needed in order to push for clarification of issues.

F. FORM FOUR GROUPS RELATED TO EACH OF THE CHAPTERS IN SECTION III OF THE BOOK (30 minutes)

1. Embrace Diversity—Chapter 8
2. Work for Equality and Justice—Chapter 9
3. Practice Forgiveness and Reconciliation—Chapter 10
4. Engage in Interfaith Dialogue and Cooperation—Chapter 11

YOUR TASKS IN EACH GROUP ARE TO:

1. Form a circle and discuss and outline the main points in your chapter.

   a. Examine the stories and share your own experiences in this key to peace.

   b. Think about ways to strengthen this key to peace in your community. What programs might you do as follow-up to this study in your church and community? List your follow-up ideas. (*Note Ideas for Church and Community Interfaith Peace Events that follow.)

   c. Think about brief sayings or slogans to convey the values and truths in interfaith peacemaking and these keys to peace. Quotations used in the textbook may also be used.

2. Move to tables, the floor, or some place where you can design and make banners, bumper stickers, posters, etc. that will show your primary messages to others. You may work in small groups or as individuals. You may also choose to write a poem or a hymn.

3. Be prepared to share your work at the beginning of the next session and perhaps to display it in your school of mission or church.

IDEAS FOR CHURCH AND COMMUNITY INTERFAITH PEACE EVENTS

1. Start an interfaith dialogue group that will meet and share faith experiences, perhaps even sponsor events and reach out to others in the community.

2. Show films, videos, and DVDs that help people understand other religions and what they stand for.

3. Invite speakers to lecture and take part in interfaith panel discussions, not only regarding their faith but also about issues of common concern such as a just society, including peace and tolerance.

4. Host a Muslim family or group for an evening meal during Ramadan, as they break fast at the end of the day. Discuss the menu so that food may be appropriate. Compare the tradition of fasting in Christianity.

5. Take small groups, including children and young people, to Jewish worship or Muslim prayers. Phone ahead to ask what you should be mindful of and to suggest your hopes for the experience.

6. Study religious holidays, seeing differences and parallels between them. Have Jewish friends, for example, discuss the meaning and practices of Passover and other holy days.

7. Have a meal that features and discusses the food of the Middle East, common to Jews and Muslims. Discuss historical, religious, health, and environmental implications of this kind of diet.

8. Plan a peace rally and invite Jewish and Muslim leaders and friends to participate.

9. Make a plan with high school and college students to set up a peace pole in your town.

10. Ask a Muslim speaker or two to speak about the impact of 9/11 and U.S. security concerns on their community.

11. Explore peacemaking in Israeli and Palestinian communities and ways to give support.

12. Examine the Patriot Act and what it means, especially for people from Muslim countries. Advocate for just legal and judicial processes for all. See if there is someone in prison for alleged offenses that you can join in supporting.

13. Organize petitions and letters to send to the White House, Congress, and local and state governments regarding issues of common concern to your interfaith community.

14. Form an interfaith delegation to meet with your city government officials or congressional representatives regarding matters of community justice and world peace.

G. REVIEW ASSIGNMENTS FOR SESSION IV

- Read Section IV, Women Engaged in Peacemaking, including the Conclusion.
- Complete your banners, bumper stickers, posters, etc. begun today and come to class early next time in order to display them around the classroom.
- Complete your autobiography of peacemaking.
- Special committees should be prepared to make presentations to the last class. To review assignments, go back to the items given at the end of Session I.

SESSON IV

WOMEN ENGAGED IN PEACEMAKING

A. STATING OUR GOALS

Connect peace, beginning with ourselves as individuals, to peace in family, community, nation, and world:

- Look at the lives of women who have been engaged in peacemaking and examine the contributions of women.
- Review a variety of groups, statements, and programs that have furthered the cause of peacemaking and interfaith understanding.
- Sum up and celebrate our learnings and our aspirations to work harder to be peace builders with people of other faiths in a pluralistic world.

B. WORSHIP AND SEEING EXHIBITS (10 minutes)

- Sing together "Let There Be Peace on Earth," *The United Methodist Hymnal*, no. 431. Have a brief moment of silent prayer from our own hearts.
- Walk around the room and look at the banners, bumper stickers, and other creations of our hearts, minds, and hands to express the values of peace.

C. BIBLE STUDY (20 minutes)
VISION IN THE PROPHETIC TRADITION

In the Tanakh or the Hebrew Bible, Micah sets forth a vision of a peaceful and pluralistic future, an image that gives hope and joy. We can imagine Jesus knowing this passage and seeking, even in the midst of the terror of the Roman occupation of his land, to build communities of shalom and connections with outsiders.

In the days to come,
The Mount of the Lord's House shall stand
Firm above the mountains;
And it shall tower above the hills.
The peoples shall gaze on it with joy,
And, many nations shall go and shall say:
"Come,
Let us go up to the Mount of the Lord,
To the House of the God of Jacob;
That He may instruct us in His ways,
And that we may walk in His paths."
For instruction shall come from Zion,
The word of the Lord from Jerusalem.
Thus He will judge among the many peoples,
And arbitrate for the multitude of nations,
however distant;
And they shall beat their swords into plowshares
And their spears into pruning hooks.
Nation shall not take up
Sword against nation;
They shall never again know war;
But [all persons] shall sit
Under [their] grapevine or fig tree
With no one to disturb [them].
For it was the Lord of Hosts who spoke.
Though all the peoples walk
Each in the names of its gods,
We will walk
In the name of the Lord our God
Forever and ever. (Micah 4:1-5, Tanakh)

United Methodist theologian Marjorie Suchocki meditates on this image in her book called *Divinity and Diversity: A Christian Affirmation of Religious Pluralism* (Nashville: Abingdon Press, 2003). She writes the following:

182

"Micah speaks of all the nations of the world streaming to Mt. Zion in order to learn the ways of God, which are just. But Micah emphasizes... that the people return to their own place, bringing with them the knowledge gained from Israel's God. Because of this knowledge, they change their ways in directions of peace....

"The nations have indeed learned the ways of peace from Mt. Zion, but they continue to follow their own religions. In today's language, they entered into dialogue, and were changed in the dialogue, even while they remained themselves. And the Jews in the text likewise remain themselves, more deeply than ever: 'We will walk in the name of the Lord our God Forever and ever' (4:5, Tanakh).

"This ancient text speaks today about the possibilities of mission as friendship, working together toward today's longings for a 'peaceable kingdom' where the nations never again will train for war. To regard the religious other as 'friend' involves us in mission together, sharing who we are, and working together for the common good. Being most deeply who we are, we are open to God's transformative call toward how we might yet be. In such openness toward the other and toward the common good, 'we will walk in the name of the Lord our God forever and ever'" (pp. 120-21).

Discuss the following questions:
1. How do you react to this vision? Can it be a reality?
2. What do we have to learn from the Abrahamic and other religions?
3. With a peaceful, just, healthy planet as our goal, are there ways that we can work together for the common good?
4. What steps can we take toward this partnership, this friendship of religious people?

D. SMALL GROUP DISCUSSION ON WOMEN AND PEACEMAKING (30 minutes)

In small groups of four or five, discuss the following questions:
1. What are women's contributions to peacemaking and interfaith cooperation? What are women's strong skills and strategies?

2. Discuss the women in the text as illustrations of peacemakers. What are their gifts? Who is your favorite and why?

3. Share autobiographies or biographies of peacemaking.

E. ORGANIZATIONS, RESOLUTIONS, AND PROGRAMS THAT MAKE FOR PEACE (up to 10 minutes each for the two reports)

1. Report on "Organizations That Contribute to Peace."
Have a list printed so that participants can take it home and add to it.

2. Report on "United Methodist Programs Related to What Makes for Peace." Here, too, a written list would be useful.

F. CLOSING WORSHIP (15-20 minutes)

Worship will be led by the Closing Worship group and the group working on the litany of "We Will Be Together."

APPENDIX

THE PEACE OF JESUS CHRIST:
A LITANY FOR WORSHIP OR DISCUSSION

ALL: The peace of Jesus is multidimensional, including all of our lives and the concerns of our world. It moves from inner peace and trust outwardly.

GROUP 1. "Let the little children come to me, and do not stop them; for it is to such as these that the kingdom of God belongs. Truly I tell you, whoever does not receive the kingdom of God as a little child will never enter it." (Luke 18:16-17)

GROUP 2. "Therefore I tell you, do not worry about your life, what you will eat, or about your body, what you will wear. For life is more than food, and the body more than clothing. Consider the ravens: they neither sow nor reap, they have neither storehouse nor barn, and yet God feeds them." (Luke 12:22-24)

GROUP 3. "Consider the lilies; how they grow: they neither toil nor spin.... If God so clothes the grass of the field, which is alive today and tomorrow is thrown into the oven, how much more will he clothe you—you of little faith!" (Luke 12:27-28)

ALL: Jesus asks us to focus on God's reign, on a world as God would like the world to be.

GROUP 1. "Do not be afraid, little flock, for it is your Father's good pleasure to give you the kingdom. Sell your possessions, and give alms. Make purses for yourselves that do not wear out, an unfailing treasure in heaven, where no thief comes near and no moth destroys. For where your treasure is, there your heart will be also." (Luke 12:32-34)

GROUP 2. "No one can serve two masters; for a slave will either hate the one and love the other, or be devoted to the one and despise the other. You cannot serve God and wealth." (Matthew 6:24)

GROUP 3. "The kingdom of God is not coming with things that can be observed; nor will they say, 'Look here it is!' or 'There it is!' For, in fact, the kingdom of God is among you." (Luke 17:20-21)

ALL: Jesus emphasizes a loving and relational world, overcoming enmity and alienation.

GROUP 1. "So when you are offering your gift at the altar, if you remember that your brother or sister has something against you, leave your gift there before the altar and go; first be reconciled to your brother or sister, and then come and offer your gift." (Matthew 5:23-24)

GROUP 2. "You have heard that it was said, 'You shall love your neighbor and hate your enemy.' But I say to you, Love your enemies and pray for those who persecute you." (Matthew 5:43-44)

GROUP 3. "So that you may be children of your Father in heaven; for he makes his sun rise on the evil and on the good, and sends rain on the righteous and on the unrighteous." (Matthew 5:45)

ALL: Jesus demonstrates compassion and teaches the ways of peace.

GROUP 1. "As he came near and saw the city, he wept over it, saying, 'If you, even you, had only recognized on this day the things that make for peace! But they are hidden from your eyes.' " (Luke 19:41-42)

GROUP 2. "You have heard that it was said, 'An eye for an eye, and a tooth for a tooth.' But I say to you, Do not resist an evildoer. But if anyone strikes you on the right cheek, turn the other also." (Matthew 5:38-39)

GROUP 3. "Blessed are the peacemakers, for they will be called children of God." (Matthew 5:9)

ALL: Jesus leaves a legacy of peace. He bridges troubled waters, breaks down dividing walls, creates a community of peace.

GROUP 1. "I will not leave you orphaned... But the Advocate, the Holy Spirit, whom the Father will send in my name, will teach you everything, and remind you of all that I have said to you. Peace I leave with you; my peace I give to you. I do not give to you as the world gives." (John 14:18, 26-27)

GROUP 2. "For he is our peace; in his flesh he has made both groups into one and has broken down the dividing wall, that is, the hostility between us.... So he came and proclaimed peace to you who were far off and peace to those who were near; for through him both of us have access in one Spirit to the Father. So then you are no longer strangers and aliens, but you are citizens with the saints and also members of the household of God." (Ephesians 2:14, 17-19)

GROUP 3. "But the wisdom from above is first pure, then peaceable, gentle, willing to yield, full of mercy and good fruits, without a trace of partiality or hypocrisy. And a harvest of righteousness is sown in peace for those who make peace." (James 3:17-18)

QUOTATIONS FROM THE ABRAHAMIC RELIGIONS

Qur'an

"The Opening
IN THE NAME OF GOD, THE COMPASSIONATE, THE MERCIFUL

All praise belongs to God,
Lord of all worlds,

the Compassionate, the Merciful,

Ruler of Judgment Day.

It is You that we worship,
and to you we appeal for help.

Show us the straight way,

the way of those You have graced,
not of those on whom is Your wrath,
nor of those who wander astray."[1]

From Romans 8:31-32

"What then are we to say about these things?
If God is for us, who is against us?
He who did not withhold his own Son,
but gave him up for all of us,
will he not with him
also give us everything else?"

Qur'an: From the Family of Imraan

"If God helps you,
then no one can overcome you;
and if God forsakes you,
who could help you then?
So let believers put their trust in God."[2]

---

[1] *The Essential Koran.* Translated and presented by Thomas Cleary. HarperSanFrancisco, 1994.

[2] Ibid.

From Deuteronomy 6:4-9

"Hear, O Israel: The Lord is our God, the Lord alone. You shall love the Lord your God with all your heart, and with all your soul, and with all your might. Keep these words that I am commanding you today in your heart. Recite them to your children and talk about them when you are at home and when you are away, when you lie down and when you rise. Bind them as a sign on your hand, fix them as an emblem on your forehead, and write them on the doorposts of your house and on your gates."

From Matthew 22:37-40

" 'You shall love the Lord your God with all your heart, and with all your soul, and with all your mind.' This is the greatest and first commandment. And a second is like it: 'You shall love your neighbor as yourself.' On these two commandments hang all the law and the prophets."

JUST WAR AND JUST PEACE

Just War

"The just-war criteria and interpretations of them have continually been shaped since the times of St. Augustine and St. Thomas Aquinas. This doctrine is meant to control and severely limit warfare. The tenets of this doctrine suggest that any and all just wars must:

- have a *just cause* seeking justice in response to serious evil;
- have a *just intention* for the restoration of peace with justice, and must not seek self-enrichment or devastation of another nation;
- be the last resort;
- have *legitimate authority* with war being declared only by a properly constituted government; and
- have a *reasonable hope of success.*

"Even more to the point in our present crisis, the just-war position suggests that if war should break out, such fighting must be constrained by two principles:

- *Discrimination:* respect is to be shown for the rights of enemy peoples and immunity given to noncombatants from direct attack.

- *Proportionality:* whereby the amount of damage inflicted must be proportionate to the ends sought. A war's harm must not exceed the war's good."

Just Peace

"The just-peace tradition is both a more 'modern assessment' and rooted in ancient commitments to nonviolence. This view suggests that a Christian's calling is to be a committed peacemaker day after day, year after year, remembering that Jesus blessed the peacemakers. Just-peace principles include such concepts as:

- *Peacemaking is a sacred calling* of the gospel, blessed by God, making us evangelists of shalom-peace that is overflowing with justice, compassion, and well-being.

- *Government is a natural institution* of human community in God's creation and a requirement for the restraint of human evil. Every policy of government must be an act of justice and must be measured by its impact on the poor, the weak, and the oppressed.

- The *transformation* of the conflict-ridden nation-state system into a new world order of common security in interdependent institutions such as the United Nations *offers the only practical hope for enduring peace.*

- *Security is not only a legitimate concern* but an imperative responsibility of governments for the protection of life and well-being.

- *All Christians*—pacifists and nonpacifists—ought to *share a strong moral presumption against violence, killing, and warfare,* seeking every possible means of peaceful conflict resolution. The gospel command to love enemies is more than a benevolent ideal. It is essential to our well-being and survival.

- *Peacemaking* in the nuclear age, under the sovereignty of the Creator God, *requires the defense of creation* itself against possible assaults that may be rationalized in the name of national defense.

- The *church of Jesus Christ,* in the power and unity of the Holy Spirit, is *called to serve as an alternative community* to an alienated and fractured world. It is therefore to be a loving and peaceable international company of disciples transcending all governments, races, and ideologies; reaching out to all enemies; and ministering to all victims of poverty and oppression."

"These principles for just peace come from an unpublished letter by United Methodist Bishop C. Dale White, who served as one of the chief drafters of the 1988 "In Defense of Creation" Bishops' pastoral letter."[3]

---

[3] From the Notes section, pp. 31–34, of the chapter "The Vocation of Peace Building" by Philip A. Amerson and John W. Woell in the book *Choosing Peace Through Daily Practices,* edited by Ellen Ott Marshall. Cleveland: The Pilgrim Press, 2005.

See also the excellent book edited by Glen Stassen on *Just Peacemaking: Ten Practices for Abolishing War.* Cleveland: The Pilgrim Press, 1998.